WAR AGAINST SILENCE AFTER TRAUMA

Unmasking and Managing The Stress Of Change

Emily Dee

Loess Hills Press
Sioux City

OTHER BOOKS BY EMILY DEE
Fun With Physical Phonics (Emily Dee Chiarello)
Souls On Board: Responses To The United Flight 232 Tragedy

Library Of Congress Catalog Number 92-75053

Dee, Emily
War Against Silence After Trauma : Unmasking
And Managing The Stress Of Change

Includes Index
1. Post-traumatic stress - - Rehabilitation
2. Crisis management 3. Aging 4. Grief **I.** Title
ISBN 0-9626818-2-2 (Hardcover)
ISBN 0-9626818-3-0 (Softcover)
616.852 1 RC552.P67

CIP-75053

First Edition

10 9 8 7 6 5 4 3 2 1

Printed in the United States of America
Acid-Free Paper

Loess Hills Press
Box 1047 Sioux City, Iowa 51102-1047

THANKS TO

the people who helped me, both emotionally and physically, while I was writing this book,

the people who told me their experiences, and

professionals trying to find solutions to their problems.

The book is their story. I just did the paper work. Because of the subject matter, in most cases I have used just first names or changed the names of people. In the case of professionals, I have included last names and topics so their reports can be located. However, I am equally grateful to all of them.

TABLE OF CONTENTS

Introduction

TWO FRIENDS

Pam Christianson and I are close friends, have been for years. We spent the afternoon together, had just parted, and were separated by a mere two miles or so on July 19, 1989, when a dramatic event in our town forced us to take a second look at our perceptions of life, our perceptions of our capabilities and our self-esteem. One traumatic day, the day the whole community became Emergency First Responders, altered our view of life, of ourselves, and propelled us both in a direction toward new lifestyles.

On that day, a giant United Airlines DC-10, Flight 232 flying from Denver to Philadelphia by way of Chicago, crashed while attempting an emergency landing, careening and spewing flames and debris in all directions. As a result of the crash at Sioux Gateway Airport in Sioux City, Iowa, an airport serving a quiet agricultural area where three states and three rivers meet, one hundred eleven people died. One hundred eighty five people lived, one died later. Our community had a Disaster Preparedness Plan in place and was able to respond effectively and humanely.

Pam's and my past training and experiences are totally different. Pam is a medical caregiver with experience in both patient care and administration. I am a writer with a degree in psychology. Gradually, we became aware that this combination of past training and experiences put us in a unique position to preserve a historical record of what took place that day before memories faded and photographs scattered. We began assembling materials for a book.

After the publication of the book, *Souls On Board: Responses To The United Flight 232 Tragedy*, was published, and again after the showing of the made-for-TV dramatization of the event *Crash Landing: The Rescue of Flight 232* staring Charlton Heston as the pilot, Richard Thomas as the Disaster Services Director and James Coburn as Sioux City's Fire Chief, we found ourselves in a spotlight of public attention. The role of a public figure isn't easy when you don't feel you've earned it, when what you do feel is that you were just doing your job. We simply did what we did before the crisis, what we are still doing after the crisis.

After the crash, we were both asked to share our stories. We both did, in an attempt to help people become aware that a disaster could happen anywhere, even in the most tranquil, pastoral setting like ours where nothing much usually happens. In other words, a disaster could happen in anybody's home town, big or small.

The community's response was credited with having saved lives. Responding efficiently and humanely to an accident is no accident. It is a consequence of behavior, the behavior of preparing ahead of time. Information learned in our community is transferable to their communities and, hopefully, can help people who are involved in emergency disaster work. Many emergency first responders have drilled extensively but have never been through an actual disaster.

Crisis Management is more than just what happens during a crisis. It includes things done

BEFORE:

Analyzing the problem and taking every possible step to avoid a disaster. Identifying and preparing skills and materials should one happen

DURING:

Not Panicking! . . . Trusting in the integrity of training and experience

AFTER:

Investing time to release Post Traumatic Stress

After *Souls On Board* was published, I got many calls from people who had read it, many of whom I didn't even know. The main question asked was: "Now that reading *Souls On Board* has made me aware of Post Traumatic Stress, what can I do to overcome it? Thus, just as calls asking:

"How did the people of a small town like Sioux City respond in such an efficient and compassionate manner to a crisis of such enormity?"

"What steps can we take to duplicate the response if such a disaster should happen in our community?"

triggered the project of writing *Souls On Board*, the question "Now that you've made me aware of Post Traumatic Stress, what can I do to overcome it?" triggered the writing of *War Against Silence After Trauma*.

The fight to make the transition from the shock and denial stage after a trauma to the stage of living in reality again is a painful one, but the inner peace after the battle is well worth it.

New scientific discoveries, made possible by development of highly sophisticated equipment, has made neuroscience (the study of the brain and how it works) a frontier in scientific investigation. Newly discovered information is having a profound effect on people's lives and on our physical health, our moods, and on our longevity. This is one of the most exciting times in history to be living because it is a time when we can all take part in, contribute to and benefit from amazing scientific investigations and discoveries.

Because scientific investigators don't stop investigating when their latest research is published, I have not referenced my sources by published reports of findings. I have, instead, referred to the work and the workers by name or topic. Librarians and most data bases locate information by name or subject. Another important source of information I have used, which you may locate by name of the investigator or by topic, is government reports. Reports of research done with taxpayers' money are available to the public. Government publications can be located by the *Superintendent of Documents Classification* (SuDoc). This system differs from the Dewey Decimal classification. SuDoc numbers begin with a letter, as in the example: A 1.10.991. The letter corresponds to an issuing agency (A=Agriculture). The next digit pertains to a subordinate department within the agency. Numbers between the decimal and colon refer to the title, and the numbers to the right of the colon give the year or issue.

Lay people have symptoms; they need solutions. Scientific investigators look for solutions; they need data on problems. With this book, I hope to continue the work Pam and I began and contribute more tiles to the mosaic of Post Traumatic Stress.

Part One—THE EXPERIENCES

Chapter I

THE DAY THE WHOLE COMMUNITY BECAME EMERGENCY FIRST RESPONDERS

Sometimes what we think we're worried about isn't what we're really worried about. Sometimes the brain keeps the truth a secret from us, putting a mask of denial and avoidance over reality that is too painful for us to handle at the moment. The shock stage after a trauma, this psychological amnesia, is helpful because it buys time for us to get strong enough to face the problem. However, it is only meant to be a temporary tool. We cannot solve and release the pain of a problem if our minds remain silent and won't tell us what it is.

The war against silence is a battle against secrets: secrets our minds hide from us and secrets society makes us keep by putting a taboo on talking about some of the events that cause trauma. Talking about tragedies often makes listeners uncomfortable so, brick by brick, a wall of silence grows around the topic. Sometimes it's done blatantly. Sometimes the wall is built in a way all can see, as during attacks against a victim during a televised court trial. Sometimes it's done more quietly, as friends' calls become less frequent and their schedules become more busy.

But, the main enemy is our own minds. When pain gets beyond the level of what we can stand, our bodies protect us by producing morphine-shaped chemicals that anesthetize us temporarily until we are stronger. Our brains give the command to silence the pain. We are liberated from the pain—but only on the conscious level. Below the conscious level, we now have a new problem to deal with. In addition to the pain of the emotions after a trauma, the conflict between reality and denial and avoidance of change has been added. Long term, these chemicals can be a factor in Post Traumatic Stress.

After a trauma, life has changed. Life has changed because our perception of what life has to hand us, of attainable goals, and of what are possible or impossible dreams has changed. Adjusting to these changes results in a period of post traumatic stress because changes produce stress. This is a painful period and our minds fight hard to avoid and protect us from it, but it is a necessary period. In addition, a fact that is often overlooked is that all changes, welcome or unwelcome, produce stress. This is often another secret our minds keep from us. Both contain elements of loss and, therefore, the pain of loss. All loss, whether from unwelcome or welcome change, must be grieved. However, like an overprotective parent, our minds often try to shield us from feeling this necessary pain.

Eventually, we must force our brains to quit hiding painful secrets. Until we acknowledge, experience and release the pain, we live with an unidentified, free-floating anxiety. We know something is wrong but we don't know what because our brain has put a mask over the cause. Conflict between denial and avoidance and reality continues.

After the trauma of having a giant DC-10 crash in my home town, I lived with this feeling of unidentified, free-floating anxiety. I lived in a state of confusion because I did not associate my pain with the terrible tragedy. I hadn't seen the victims, nor was I a first responder involved with the total devastation of that day. At the time, I did not understand the dynamics of the secondary trauma nor that I, too, was a victim.

At the time, I did not understand how experiences in the present release stored emotions that were not grieved after traumas in the past. I now know, though I didn't then, that emotions from experiences in my past had been released and were at work in my body stimulating feelings and reactions to experiences in the present. Feelings of helplessness, of abandonment and loss from deaths of loved ones in the past, loss of my perception of how I thought life would continue to be all were contributing to my anxiety and restlessness. I lived with an underlying feeling of doom. At the time, I didn't realize it stemmed from a thought my subconscious mind was playing over and over again. "This terrible thing happened once, it could happen again."

It is important that we unmask and face the reality of events that are causing us pain. It is not only important for us individually, it is also important because these chemicals are a factor in many of the ways some people are using to mask the pain of changes that have taken place in their lives. The role of these chemicals in ways such as addictions, compulsive behavior, rigidity, controlling, promiscuity or workaholism, is not understood. Until the role of these chemicals is understood, many of the problems of our country, and countries all over the world, will not be understood—or solved.

July 19, 1989 changed my life, as it did the life of my friend Pam Christianson, and the lives f thousands of others. That was the day the Siouxland community—and the world—learned that it was the home of a thousand heroes. What is heroism? Heroism is a reaction to our ecology. Our ecology is our relationship with plants, animals, and people around us. Each new experience changes it because it changes this relationship. Our ecology affects production of chemicals in the brain that control mood, productivity, and behavior. These chemicals, called neuromessengers, transmit subliminal messages without our being aware of it on the conscious level. These neuromessengers are involved in Post Traumatic Stress. Trauma means injury. Post Traumatic Stress can result from either physical or emotional injury. It puts a glass ceiling on our productivity and happiness level, a barrier we can't see but can't rise above. Until the role of these chemicals is understood, many problems in our lives, in our personal productivity, and in our society today can not be understood—or solved.

When a cockpit crew of four in a severely disabled United Airlines DC-10 and five airport tower controllers succeeded in guiding the giant plane into the Sioux Gateway Airport, it was fortunate because the community had a Disaster Preparedness Plan and people trained to carry it out. The Siouxland Response to the United Flight 232 Tragedy, as it has now become known in places all over the world, was not due to the fact that so many people showed up to help at the crash site. It was the fact that they knew what to do when they got there.

Our community's relationship with nature is an important influence in our lives and an important thread in the tapestry of what happened that day. Ecology is not just something we read about in newspapers or learn about on TV through programs showing the destruction of rain forests in South America. The Siouxland Response was a dramatic expression of our partnership with nature and of the ecology of the community. Because we are an agriculture-based community, this connection with nature is a part of the spirit of the people. People and plants germinate here, grow, develop, and die. It is all considered part of nature's cycle. We don't turn away in denial from any phase of life, each is accepted. It is not an acceptance that we don't fight. We fight to make life as lengthy as possible. We fight to live the highest quality of life we can, too. We embrace each part of the cycle, clasp it in our arms and press it to our bosoms.

We accept each part of the life cycle, and we give it our best shot. Because the prospect of death doesn't overwhelm and immobilize us, we have the freedom to plan for it. We can use our energies to visualize and design plans to deal with it and to deal with the possibility that it might happen unexpectedly and tragically. People were able to handle human injury—fractures, concussions, skin tears and bruises—because they had previously faced and accepted the fact that such a thing, though certainly not very likely, could in fact happen in our home town. Because people had planned and trained, they knew what to do and how to do it when they got to the crash site.

They knew how to do it because the plan calls for a yearly drill. The first Disaster Drill from this plan, written by then Director of the Woodbury County Sheriff's Emergency Operations Center, Jeff Trometer, and continued and expanded by his successor Gary Brown, was held in September 1983. The scenario involved a traffic accident on Interstate 29. In October of 1987, that year's training exercise was held at almost the exact spot of the crash of Flight 232. It simulated a major disaster—"a commercial airliner which had crashed shortly after takeoff, scattering its 130 occupants to the grass and pavement below." The day of the actual crash, the first survivor reached the hospital seven miles away in 17 minutes after impact, all survivors were cleared out of the crash site within 48 minutes, and of the 296 people aboard the plane, 186 were still alive.

Preparedness saved lives. People who are in unity with nature and the cycle of life and death create results that are in unity with the cycle of life and death. When a disaster happens, they can deal with the situation as a natural one. This inner harmony results in responses that are effective and humane.

However, people in our community as well as those connected by TV, radio and newspaper reports, paid a price afterwards—the same price that professional emergency first responders always have to pay. They were left with memories of the sights, sounds and smells of the day firmly encoded on their brains. The event came and went, but the memory of it and, for many, emotions stored at the time, will remain a tangible part of the brain. Emotions are stimulated by physical chemicals. During times of crisis, it is the brain's job to produce these neuromessengers.

The things people experienced that day produced a whole lot of neuromessengers. All of a sudden, the population of a civilian community, and those involved through media reports, found themselves surrounded by the sounds and sights of a war zone. Some estimates put the number of first response rescue workers who were on the scene at the airport when the plane crashed at 700. Though trained, most of those people were emotionally unprepared for what they saw.

Although no one can ever be fully prepared for the level of emotional and physical agony and suffering this civilian population suddenly found itself a part of, soldiers sent into a war zone at least have been given some exposure to what to expect. They are made aware of what a war zone is like. They are taught skills for handling stress and are rehearsed (drilled) by actually being given a chance to role play different scenarios of things that might happen. At the crash of Flight 232, the explosive activity of the brain spewing out such a frenzy of messages clogged up brain systems. What the emergency workers were hearing, seeing and smelling elicited responses of horror, just absolute horror. Many people's minds went on overload and blocked out what was going on. The word emotion comes from the Greek e, meaning exit, and moveo. Just like molecules of blood on the ambulances will not go away unless effort is spent to scrub it off, blocked molecules of emotions will not go away without effort. Unless emotions are experienced and moved out, they remain there like cobwebs in the warehouses of people's brains.

Stored feelings can cause other pain too because experiences in the present trigger emotions from past experiences. When these stored emotions bubble up, they can get attributed to an event in the present rather than the past trauma. Wounds can never heal because the focus is on the present trauma as the cause rather than the real cause. Once feelings get pushed under, they become a much harder problem to work with because they then enter the area of subliminal messages a person is not even aware of on the conscious level. However, even though harder to do, they can still be released.

The crash of Flight 232 changed my life because it forced me to take a new look at my values and at what is actually important in my life. The emotions of being totally helpless and unable to control, or even influence, the events taking place around me forced me to go back and look at events in my childhood with the eyes of an adult, rather than the immature eyes of the tiny child and adolescent I was when the events occurred. I could see, and my body could feel, similarities. As an adult, however, my perception was that I had the resources to get past this period of helplessness. When experiences in the present trigger blocked emotions from experiences in the past and the two do not mesh, our brains force us to run the two conflicting perceptions through a reality check, acknowledge which is true, and grieve the loss of the unrealistic belief before we feel peace again.

The emotions I experienced as a result of the plane crash triggered a chain of perceptions that completely altered my self-image, and therefore my life. Experiences alter self-image and self-image determines personal productivity. We only succeed in projects we think we can accomplish. If we have no hope of succeeding we don't even try, don't try hard enough, or don't try long enough. There are no successful endings to projects that aren't started.

At the time of the crash, I had an extremely negative self-image of myself and my capabilities. This self-image had been molded by two major forces. I was grieving the loss of a thirty-year marriage, and I had been trained by my culture in childhood to believe that a female could not fill her own physical needs. Being raised in a culture that divided tasks into men's work and women's work, I was deliberately taught, as were men, that I could only fill 50% of my needs. I saw myself lacking the ability to provide even my basic food and shelter.

It was not a realistic self-image. I had three college degrees, one published book, and a new manuscript which was in the hands of an agent and receiving encouraging comments. I had won two national Department of Energy contests for solar energy designs and had been very successful in my role as wife and mother-in-the-home of three sons and extension of my husband in his career as a music conductor. Problem is, our brain does not function on reality. Our brain is fueled by our self-image's *perception* of reality. Although unrealistic, it was my self-image, not reality, that was in control. Depression and fear were controlling my life. Although going through all the motions needed to carry me through my life, I was a member of an army of the walking dead.

Although Pam and I had been together in the airport area earlier in the day and the plane had gone over my head two and a half miles before impact, I was unaware of the catastrophe. My mind is not trained, as hers is, to process signs of emergency. I am now aware that my mind has been trained just the opposite. Because I live a block from one of the hospitals and the sound of air ambulances over my house are a part of my life, I have trained my mind to block out the sounds of emergency so I can live a normal life. When I am writing on a project, I write from 4 am to noon. Because I get up so early, I take a nap in the afternoon. July 19, 1989, was no exception. I was asleep when my son called. Mario often calls me when he sees something on TV he thinks I would be interested in.

MARIO: Mom, are you all right?"

EMILY: Sure, I'm all right. Why shouldn't I be?

MARIO: Well, I just saw something on national news that I think you should be watching. They told about a terrible plane crash at the airport in Sioux City.

EMILY: What kind of plane, Mario?

MARIO: I don't know because I wasn't really watching, but the set was on in the room. I saw this terrible fireball, so whatever it was, it was a big one, a really big one Mom. Go turn on the TV. I bet they'll show it again on the local news.

Later Frank, my oldest son, called. He's a flyer in Japan.

FRANK: Mom, you all right?

EMILY: Yeah.

FRANK: We're going wild in the office over here. That pilot couldn't have done what he did. Nobody can fly a plane when they've lost all hydraulics. Mom, send anything you can get your hands on that tells about that. Nobody in this office believes it. We're flyers. We know it can't be done.

My youngest son, who was studying electronics in Denver, checked on me next.

PAUL: We were watching the news and saw what happened with that plane. A lot of people here are studying aeronautics, and they are all talking about that flight pattern and how the pilot got the plane to Sioux City. The men in the control tower were fantastic.

It seemed like the entire world was focusing on my small midwestern city. I dressed and went out to the airport, by now crowded with media people. Reporters and photographers recording the tragedy and sending the information out to newspapers, radio and TV stations all over the world were already there. Many had their tripods set up atop huge vans to be able to shoot over the top of the tall security fence around the runways. They were to stay there for a week and to be joined by crews from as far away as Tokyo and South America.

My mind anesthetized me from the devastation of the tragedy. Just the month before, I had taken a week-long photography course at a lodge high in the Rocky Mountains. So, I had just been taught to look for things in my neighborhood that would tell an interesting story on film. As bizarre as it seems to me now, the thought that went through my mind was: "There's no use taking a picture from this angle. There's nothing to be seen from here except a piece of the nose cone and a big swath of black, burned grass." Of course, that was the point.

Chemicals produced by my brain were protecting me by anesthetizing me from feeling more pain than I could handle at the moment. When I saw that fireball on TV, my emotions shut down. The horror of the pain and agony those flames represented was too much for me to handle. I know now, though I didn't then, that when pain gets beyond the threshold of what we can handle our body produces morphine-like chemicals. Because of newly developed, highly sophisticated diagnostic equipment, scientists are now learning about the role of neuromessengers. There are two types of neuromessengers, exciter neuromessengers and inhibitor neuromessengers. Scientists have now found a complete system in our bodies that they didn't know about before. In addition to our skeletal system, muscular system, etc., they have now discovered an opiate system. Neuromessenger molecules, some with the same shape as morphine molecules, travel through our bodies. When they find receptor sites with mirror images of their own, these opiates plug in and carry out the work of anesthetizing us to all pain too intense for us to bear at the moment. Opiates produced inside my own body were protecting me at the crash site.

My work was not to be at the crash site, but rather to start the next day as a volunteer in downtown Sioux City manning the office of a United States senator. I was asked to free his staff to work in the makeshift morgue set up in a hanger at the airport. The Senator's office was used as a communications center. People were harried as information from various government agencies flowed in and out through that point. Because I get up so early I go to bed early, so I left the crash site when it began to get dark. The airport lies between two natural barriers, the river on one side and a row of loess hills on the other. Loess is wind-deposited silt. There are only two places in the world that these unique land forms exist at such depths, here along the Missouri River and on mainland China. As I drove along the interstate, I noticed a conflict in my mind. Part of me wanted to look out toward the river to the crash site to see the tragedy from a different angle, but another part wanted to draw my eyes to the soft curves of the rolling hills on the other side of the highway as they were lit up in the gentle light of dusk. It was not until later that I was helped to understand about dissociation. Dissociation is the mind's way of protecting a person from too much pain by removing him or her from the horror of a situation. My mind kept trying to pull me back to a happier time when I had stood in the archeological museum in Xian, China, as the same type of crumbly silt was being carefully dusted away and a whole army of Qin Warrior pottery figures were being uncovered.

By the time I got home, a feeling of numbness had come over me. I sat motionless as the dusk gradually turned into darkness. The only thing that broke through my daze was a phone call from a supportive friend working as a counselor in Beverly Hills, California. Even though there were few words spoken, I was aware of a warmth generated by her emotional support. I didn't even turn on the TV that night. I knew the pictures would come back to me later if I did. I didn't need to see the TV version. I felt I saw the play with the original sets.

I know now that, after I saw that fireball, my body produced inhibitor neuromessengers that allowed me to emotionally detach from the pain. I went through all the physical motions expected of me, but felt no feelings. Pam's body, on the other hand, produced exciter neurotransmitters that energized her into action. Her brain immediately analyzed what her plan of action should be and what clothing and supplies she would need. She went home, prepared for action, then went to the crash site and took action. She talked about it later.

PAM: I've done a lot of thinking about your friend Bob's reaction. He remarked that everybody was making a big deal over how lucky it was that the disaster rescue team had a twenty minute call to get prepared and in place before the plane crashed. I remember he said he didn't think that was enough time.

BOB: How can anybody get prepared and in place in twenty minutes? I couldn't even get out of the house in twenty minutes. First I'd have to go to the bathroom. Then there'd be a few things I'd have to finish in the kitchen before I could leave.

EMILY: . . . and if I thought I was going to be gone for a few days, I'd surely have to water the plants before I left.

BOB: Don't first response workers go to the bathroom before they leave, or is it written in the Disaster Plan: Go to the bathroom every hour on the hour so you'll be prepared?

PAM: That makes an interesting point. People whose life experiences have trained them to react with action in time of crisis not only RESPOND differently to a disaster, they even THINK differently than other people do. As author and researcher Norman Cousins points out, people who are trained ahead of time to view a crisis as a challenge react to it as an energizing rather than immobilizing experience.

I didn't go to the bathroom. You and I had attended a meeting that started at 1 o'clock. From there I went directly to see a patient, then, I picked up my kids at my mom's. I hadn't been to the bathroom all afternoon. As I was driving out to the airport I thought: "I need to go to the bathroom." That was the last time I thought of it until I got home that night about six or seven hours later. My mind just blocked all thoughts of body functions, food or, except in rare moments, exhaustion.

I just turned into a machine.

Chapter II

MY SELF-IMAGE WAS ALTERED BUT NATURE IS MY MENTOR

After the crisis was over, Pam and I were both left with self-images and images of our ecology that didn't mesh with those we had before the crash. During the emergency we were asked to do things that were far beyond our comfort zones. Things needed to be done, and they needed to be done fast. There was a Disaster Preparedness Plan but, because of the enormity of the disaster, the numbers overwhelmed the plan. People who had trained and drilled to do specific jobs now had to become a skeleton of leadership and people from the community (with no experience in doing these tasks) were suddenly needed to flesh it out. Local people had no time to analyze whether they had a college degree in this, whether they had two year's experience, or even whether they had natural ability. There were jobs that obviously had to be done, had to be done fast, and people were asked to do them.

After several weeks, the intense pressure generated by the crash and follow-up activities died down. Pam and I were left with feelings we couldn't identify, uneasy feelings that made us confused and anxious. My surroundings were the same; the trauma had not physically touched my life. I lived in the same house, ate the same food, and followed the same routine. But, my life was different. I was jumpy, anxious, depressed. There was an underlying feeling of doom. I now know that this is a typical symptom of Post Traumatic Stress. It is a feeling of

"This terrible thing happened once, it could happen again." My life alternated between anxiety and numbed silence. I couldn't pinpoint why I felt such a war going on inside me.

I know now, but I didn't then, that there was a chemical basis for this stress. The inner conflict was a result of the way memories are stored. Our minds work like a computer. As memories are being stored, experiences in the present scan back and forth for their proper pigeonhole in the brain. They trigger emotions and memories of experiences in the past. If a present perception conflicts with a stored perception, tension is produced. This tension will not ease until the realistic parts of each memory mesh into a new perception based on the reality of what actually happened in each experience.

The process we go through to resolve this inner war of conflicting memories not only results in relief from the pain of inaccurate memories, it also results in inner growth. During times of crisis, our bodies often produce more neuromessengers than can be moved out of the body. If some get stuck, these chemicals can cause the body's regular chemical balance to get out of balance. This imbalance produces tension. To get relief from this tension, we revert back to patterns of behavior that have worked for us in the past. People use the skills their experiences have taught them to use. Unfortunately, some people have had bad experiences (and therefore bad training). The patterns of behavior they have developed are dysfunctional. They don't function in a way that can bring happiness.

Just as we need the right balance of chemicals in our body, we need the right balance in the three areas of our body: mind (the intellectual area), body (the physical area) and soul (our feelings and emotions). If too much focus is put on one area, it looms larger than the others. Like a boot on a tire, it causes our wheel of life to run bumpy.

For a while after the crash it was easy to isolate myself in my home. I continued working on my writing, rarely speaking to anyone. Pam, for a change, seemed to withdraw inside herself. Eventually, as I often do when things get out of harmony in my life, I retreated to nature. To me, the cause and consequences system of nature is the fixed center of a changing and troubled world. The world may change, but the system doesn't. I often find myself insulated from, and sometimes forget, the dependability of the system . . . but it's always there. More importantly it, rather than I, controls my life.

Nature is my mentor and, when my life gets out of control, I go back and check out the system. When I first arrive in the wild, I am not in harmony with it because the very disharmony of my life is what has driven me back for guidance.

I am a hiker. At first I am propelled by nervous energy, trashing through a sea of prairie flowers or clamoring clumsily up a mountain. Just as flowers in the wild harmonize with their surroundings, chemicals produced in our brains that govern mood and behavior respond to our environments. Ecology and physiology are inseparably intertwined. In response to a stimulus, (either external like a view or event, or internal like a perception or thought), our brains produce neuromessengers—the chemicals that transmit instructions throughout our bodies.

When I hike, I function in the physical area. Often as I leave the structure of civilization behind and cross a variety of terrain, I become more aware of the variety of terrain also available to me in the intellectual and emotional areas of my life. Just as I come upon surprises along the trail, I realize that by breaking down the personal barriers built up from my perceptions of past experiences I can find surprises in the emotional and intellectual areas. I realize that my life can be more in balance, more productive and rewarding.

I return from the wild with a clearer understanding that my fascination with life rests on meshing the lessons of the wild and civilization. I need both, and I need them in balance. Only then can I live with stress without distress and balance on my shoulders the weight of life's patches of rain with the lightness of solutions of life's patches of sunshine.

> The balance of mind, body, and soul is the
> fuel of harmony and the power of hope.
> I understand that more clearly when I
> am enveloped in nature's system of cause
> and consequences.

After the crash, I retreated to nature by joining a group taking down a barbed-wire fence on the Niobrara Nature Preserve, a bison preserve on the Niobrara River in Nebraska. The herd had been enlarged, so new fences had to be put up to enlarge their area too. Our group's job was to take down the old fence. I wasn't comfortable with the idea that we were working inside the newly-fenced area on the same side with the bison. Since I was the only woman in the group, at night I slept in a bunkhouse by myself. I was scared to death. I knew the porcupine was outside because we had passed him when Al, the preserve manager, walked me back to the bunkhouse in the dark after supper. But, I wasn't sure about mice and things. When I called to volunteer he had asked

AL: How do you feel about mice?

EMILY: Mice?

AL: Well, I usually ask city people, because mice get in the walls of some of our sleeping quarters here.

EMILY: I would prefer one without mice.

Since then, the ranch staff and volunteers have used donated materials (probably from donors who had slept in quarters with mice in the walls) to build two new bunkhouses for visiting investigators and volunteers and an Education Outreach Center with displays of fossils found on the preserve.

I enjoyed being outdoors tromping around on the prairie, riding in a pick-up to see a prairie dog town or to check out an old wind charger. As I moved around using muscles I don't often use, my circulation improved. I noticed the tension drain from my body, and I began to relax. I was not aware at that time that there is a type of mental health therapy, Movement Therapy, based on this physical release of tension. I just knew I was moving around, having fun and feeling good.

I learned to pull staples out of a fence post, how to roll up rusty barbed wire and, on the very last day, how to toss my own roll of barbed wire up on the back and drive a four-wheel drive pick-up to the dump site. In the evenings, there was time to hike down through the trees to the river. Eastern and western plant species overlap at the preserve and so do northern and southern species. As the altitude changed along the trail, I could see plants in a succession from water hungry river bottom reeds, through cedar and birch trees all the way to dry prairie grasses at the highest point. I had needed a change from my usual surroundings, and that place sure was.

My plan was to come home Friday as Pam had a Family Reconstruction scheduled for Saturday in Sioux City. A Family Reconstruction is a powerful psychological tool developed by Virginia Satir, author, therapist and international educator. I had signed up as one of her supportive friends. Thursday night I was called away from the dinner table to take a telephone call from her. I seldom give anyone my number when I run away from home to re-establish my roots in nature. However, I knew Pam was having to deal with some extremely emotional issues as she prepared for this confrontation with reality, so I left an emergency number with her. I wanted her to have the option of drawing strength from our friendship if she felt she needed to.

Virginia Satir was a pioneer in recognizing the influence the role that family dynamics has on a person's perception of reality. Rather than being based on truth, a child's perception of reality is molded by life rules imprinted on its neural pathway at an early age by its family and the family's social structure. A child's perception of reality is molded by the way its family talks, thinks, and acts. Satir is most remembered for

her pioneering work in focusing attention
on the role of family dynamics,

her belief that the self-esteem of the client
or the client's family shouldn't be destroyed
by the processes used in the therapy,

drawing attention to the effect of being raised
in an hierarchy system, the effect it has on a
person's self-image,

and the powerful psychological tool she
developed called Family Reconstruction.

In the Family Reconstruction process, a person collects as much information as possible about his or her family tree and looks carefully at the behavior of his or her ancestors. As an adult, it is possible to see the family's history with adult eyes rather than the immature eyes of a child. It is also possible to see the family's dynamics, such as personalities, patterns of relating, recognizable roles assigned by the family (consciously or unconsciously) to its members, cultural background, and significant events.

Pam had spent the last six or so months collecting information about her family. While I was going the physical route, Pam was going the intellectual route. This was a switch from our normal roles. When things get too painful, my usual pattern is to flip into intellectual, her's to revert to physical. She is an energetic workaholic and, when there is no more work to do, her attitude is "Let's party! Let's flirt! Let's stir up some diversionary action here so we don't have to feel the pain."

PAM: After the crash, I retreated into my mind. I threw myself into the job of gathering information for my Family Reconstruction. At the time, my husband and I were in counseling because there were serious problems with our marriage. We had reached the point where it was necessary to step back from each other and take an objective look at our relationship. I was becoming aware that many of the problems I was having in my life were actually being caused by my reaction to experiences in my childhood rather than what was happening in my marriage. I was beginning to see the relationship between my habits and behaviors and my traumas in childhood. Experiences in my past (even experiences I had blocked out from my conscious mind) were setting me up to be revictimized in the present.

Our plan was for my husband to get an apartment. We would share the time with the children by alternating. I'd have them one week, he the next. I discussed it with Emily.

EMILY: Pam, the fact that you and your husband need time and space away from each other isn't the kids' fault. They shouldn't be penalized by having to give up their home every other week. If you two need a change, you do the changing.

PAM: That made sense, so I lived in the home with my kids one week and at Emily's the next, alternating with my husband who lived with the kids one week and in a college dorm the next. The weeks I was living at Emily's, I worked hard on researching my family tree for the Family Reconstruction. I picked a little garret room with an old-fashioned window seat. I spread pictures out all over the place. I spread out pictures of my parents, their parents, houses they had lived in, and family group pictures from many generations. I made up posters of their habits and characteristics and lots of comparison charts.

Now, Pam was calling me at the nature preserve to tell me that at this point, two days before the date, it had to be canceled. Not enough people had signed up because it had unknowingly been scheduled in conflict with an important event in our town. Through the weeks of preparation, her feelings had been elevated to an emotional high as she relived so many events of her past. Now, the emotions had no outlet. Although there was a logical explanation (and Pam's mind could accept it intellectually) her emotions were not able to process the pain of such a disappointment and they shut down. A blanket of silence fell over the whole topic. Her schedule became "too busy" to attend the group sessions and she soon dropped out completely.

After talking with Pam, I went back to the dinner table but I had missed most of the mealtime. I had been invited to meet Carolyn and Mario, a couple who were there doing research on the bison, because Carolyn is an author too. She told me that she had supported herself while a college student by writing human interest articles for newspapers. She thought I might enjoy that and suggested I check it out. That seemed interesting, so on the drive home I began putting my thoughts together.

I often get some of my best thoughts while driving through the countryside. I keep a tape recorder in the car and record thoughts as they hit me. On the drive back, I wandered around back roads instead of traveling the well-traveled path. By the time I got home, I had the outline formed for a newspaper human interest story. Because Pam and I often meet to bounce ideas off each other, the next morning I called and suggested we meet for brownies at a little bakery.

PAM: At ten o'clock in the morning, Emily?

I'm a chocoholic. At that time, I compulsively ate a brownie at four o'clock every afternoon. Because I asked her to meet me at ten o'clock in the morning, she could tell that this was a serious brownie eating meeting so she hurried on over. I told her about my plan to write a human interest story. She was excited and offered to help me collect materials because she saw an additional reason for putting the information on paper.

PAM: Emily, I've just been asked to make a speech about the crash at the National Convention of Military Surgeons in San Diego. That would make a wonderful reference hand-out for them to take home.

EMILY: We'll write it together. We'll be co-authors.

PAM: I'm not an author.

EMILY: I am. I'll put the information on paper.

Working on the project was great fun. As we got into it, we realized it was much more than a newspaper article so we changed the focus. As we both gathered information, and I put it on paper, it became clear that the project was more important than a hand-out. What was developing was a historical account of what happened that day in our town. We were assembling and organizing information and pictures before they got scattered and lost. Again, our focus changed. The format changed from reference hand-out to book format.

With the decision to search for the reality of what happened during the tragedy, Pam and I made the first step out of the shock stage of trauma. To work on the project, we had to talk about the details. We could no longer deny and avoid the emotions triggered by the event in the present. In order to write an accurate historical account, we had to face both the reality of the event and of our own emotions. We had to break the silence we had fallen into after the trauma.

We were a great team! Neither one of us could have pulled the project off alone because the emotions it triggered were too painful. Alone, we would have quit rather than face them. As we worked together we had to negotiate, and mesh, our two wildly different—and often conflicting—styles. There were battles, some of them pretty fierce. Strangely, our battles didn't alienate us from each other but tended to draw us closer. I know now, though I didn't then, that this emotion was, in fact, a vital ingredient that was needed to round out and give balance to our project—and to our friendship.

As we worked together, we discovered that the experience in the present triggered emotions of experiences in the past. Sometimes the way we had reacted at the time of the past experience held little similarity to the way we were reacting in this experience. Often we had to take time out from the writing to resolve a difference in self-images before it was possible to continue.

As the book evolved, a new self-image also evolved for each of us, but I was not aware of that at the time. As my self-image became stronger, my writing became stronger. I began to see the project as a greater and greater challenge, and my brain produced more and more exciter chemicals. I was writing the story; Pam was helping me gather the materials. We were a team. I wanted both names on the book. Pam would not go along with the idea.

PAM: Emily, you're the writer.

EMILY: Yes, but we are doing the project together. I couldn't do this by myself, and even if I tried, it would not be the same project. Your part is very important.

PAM: Emily, it is the person who puts the words on paper who is the author. I often ask you for feedback on medical matters because I know you give me a different slant, a slant I might be too closely involved in to see. But, when it comes to making a decision, or giving a shot, you are not the one who does it. I am. I am the medical caregiver.

I recently went back and asked Pam to talk to me about some of her emotions at the time. As we did for that book, we walked or sat for hours with a tape recorder running as we flushed out memories and details.

EMILY: You made some drastic changes in your life after the crash, Pam. Talk about your process for deciding to make those changes.

PAM: I think it was during triage that I actually made the decision to make the major changes I later made in my life.

EMILY: In triage? You were thinking about it in triage? Don't you mean after it was over and you had time to think?

PAM: No, in triage. I just kinda looked around and I thought "My God, so many people's lives ended here today. I wonder if they told the people they loved how they felt before they left." It was at the crash site, among the dead and wounded, that it became very clear to me that the little stuff just doesn't matter. What matters is to follow your heart. You need to do what you truly want to do in your heart. For better than six years, my heart had wanted to move to Colorado. I think I decided right there to move to Colorado.

After it was all over, I guess the new self-image that I saw was of a person who had made a difference that day, and the type of person who could make a difference in life. For some reason, I thought that the Air Force had a bigger picture than what I had seen as a nurse in Sioux City. I realized that the Air Force could be my facilitator to getting to the goal that I wanted, which was to live in Colorado. So, I used it as a vehicle. I bargained with them.

EMILY: Yes, I remember. I was surprised at that, because I guess I'd never seen anybody negotiate with the military and just frankly tell them what her needs were and what she had to have in order to join. I'd only seen it from the side of the military telling a person what they needed, and cutting orders that filled their needs regardless of what the person's needs were. Frankly, I was amazed.

You told them what base you wanted (you made it clear you meant only one base), what date you wanted to go in (based on your three children's needs), and what pay was the least you would need to fill your and your children's needs.

PAM: Yes but I made up my budget from what I knew about in Iowa. It was different in Colorado. I made a mistake on that budget and I had to work weekends as a nurse in the hospital in town to supplement it.

EMILY: That's not my point.

PAM: Well, it turned out to be an important point for me at six thirty some Saturday mornings.

So, I used the Air Force Academy as a vehicle to get me to where I wanted to be in life. I bargained with them, basically. I said "I will go to work for you for three years if you will agree to get me to the geographic location where I want to be in life."

They did, and I went. That was what my heart wanted. I was bored and felt stagnated in Sioux City. It was not because of where I was living, but I wanted to blame it on that. I needed a major life change, so instead of just spinning my wheels and talking about it, I decided I would take action.

What the crash made me realize was that you never know how long you are going to live—how long you are going to be on this earth. So, if you can make a difference, then quit spinning your wheels and do it. The difference I needed to make was for me. It was not for anybody else, just for me.

So I decided: Just do it. You see, what I had always done was what everybody else wanted me to do. I had been the good daughter who always stayed in the vicinity of the family, the sister who was always there for somebody to talk to and, to a certain extent, the person who was always the mediator for my family. I was the one they came to resolve family conflicts. Although people had told me this before, I couldn't really see it when I was there. Now it is becoming more and more apparent to me the longer I am gone. The first year I was in Colorado I spent a lot of time on the phone, trying to negotiate, trying to arbitrate. I finally gave up that role. When I did, my family began to see it too, and they admitted it. When my family finally gave up on the idea that I was always going to be there, they had to look among themselves to fill their own needs. To a certain extent I've lost a lot of their respect because I choose not to play that role any more. I think they probably feel I have abandoned them.

EMILY: I see your motivation for moving, but you made three major changes in one week, if I remember correctly. You quit your job, sold your house, and left your husband.

PAM: And moved 700 miles.

EMILY: Okay. Four major changes. Prioritize them.

PAM: Prioritize them?

EMILY: Yeah. Tell me how in the world you made those decisions, and which one you made first. None of them fit into your old self-image. Let's back up. At the crash you realized there was more to life than you were experiencing.

PAM: No. What I realized was that I really needed to follow my heart and quit wishing that I would. I did not want to go through life and, at the end, look back and say "I wish I would have." It's that motto of: Just do it.

EMILY: Okay, so you had your goal then: to follow your heart. What in the world did you do first? You quit your job first, didn't you?

PAM: Yes, but I already had another job lined up. My first decision was to move to Colorado, so the 700 mile move was the first one. Then I had to find a way out there. The Air Force would move me, and give me a job, so that's two down.

EMILY: Okay, but there are still some details like a husband and three kids.

PAM: My husband and I had known for a long time that our marriage was wrong, but it can sometimes be easier to live together than to admit it and take action. I knew the time had come to take action.

EMILY: So, you accepted when the Air Force Academy offered to fly you to Colorado in a jet for an interview.

PAM: Yes. That was one of the worst experiences in my life. It was a small plane and we hit a storm. There was an extended period before we got into Colorado Springs when I honestly thought the other passengers and I were going to die. It was shortly after the crash of Flight 232, and it just seemed to me like a repeat. I've had a number of bad experiences where the sights and smells of Flight 232 came back to me as vividly as they were that day. That was one of them.

EMILY: Yes. I also remember one night when you called me in a panic. You didn't think you were going to be able to keep your job because of flashbacks from Flight 232.

PAM: Yes. People at the Air Force Academy are required to take ongoing training to stay certified. I was taking a required course. One class was training for treating patients after an airline crash. When they started bringing the patients into triage, I just freaked out. I knew I couldn't pass the class and I didn't think I could keep my job if I didn't pass it.

EMILY: I remember that.

PAM: I didn't lose my job . . the feeling of panic either.

EMILY: The other incident I remember was when a United Airlines plane crashed in Colorado Springs, where you were living. When I heard it on the news, I knew you would be upset. I called but couldn't get in touch with you right away.

PAM: I panicked again. I felt I was jinxed, and that United had followed me and had another crash because I was living there. In my mind I knew my thinking was not logical but I had tremendous guilt feelings that I had caused the crash.

EMILY: I worried about what might happen if you had to be sent to the crash site.

PAM: I didn't need to go to the crash site. There were no survivors, so they needed no nurses.

Chapter III

THE PILOT'S FAMILY WAS ABLE TO MOVE INCOGNITO IN AN UNFAMILIAR AREA

Meanwhile, as Pam and I were working on the book and struggling through our emotions in Sioux City, a lady we did not know, but who would eventually be a part of our lives, was struggling through her emotions in another part of the country. Darlene Haynes, the wife of the pilot who headed the team that guided the giant plane onto the grounds of the airport, was feeling the emotions of the secondary trauma of the tragedy. In any disaster, two traumatic events take place simultaneously, the primary trauma and the trauma experienced by family, friends, and workers dealing with the dead, injured or dysfunctional. The physical and emotional trauma of the first group and the emotional trauma of the second group can be equally devastating. Both can have a long term effect on the lives of people involved unless effectively dealt with at the time of the event. I recently had a chance to talk with her about it. Our working together on this book came about through a strange series of coincidences.

There were major problems with the cover of the book *Souls On Board*. There seemed to be no way out of the problem and I was at my wits end. One day I was driving down the street, practically in tears, when I passed the studio of a photographer in town. I thought, "His work is some of the best I have ever seen, and I've lived a lot of places and seen a lot of photographers' work. I bet he'd know what to do." Impulsively,

I wheeled the car over to the curb, shoved a quarter in the meter, and stormed in. I had never met the man, but I had seen pictures of him. I recognized him standing there in the reception room. I thrust the book in his hand.

EMILY: There's trouble with the cover of a book I wrote. What would you do if you had this problem?

GEORGE: You wrote this book? I just bought six copies of it last week to give to some people. I wish I had known you were in the area, I'd have had you autograph them.

He not only had an experienced eye that could recognize the problem, he knew who had the skills to correct it. After suggesting some people I could call, he asked:

GEORGE: Do you have time to talk?

EMILY: Yes.

We went into his conference room. We talked a long time and, as the conversation developed, we found we had a lot in common.

GEORGE: Out of respect, some people and I from Sioux City made reservations and flew on Capt. Haynes' last flight with United Airlines, his retirement flight on August 26, 1991. When he reached the mandatory retirement age of sixty he had to stop flying. A lot of people felt the same way we did and booked seats on the flight—friends, survivors and families of Flight 232. At the retirement dinner the night before, I sat next to Darlene Haynes and she talked about her feelings. She has a story that needs to go in your new book about Post Traumatic Stress.

EMILY: Do you think she'd be willing to tell it to me?

GEORGE: Yes. They're coming to Sioux City in April. I'll introduce you to her.

I thanked him, but I did not plan to pursue it. I had made the commitment to exhibit the book at the American Booksellers Association Convention in May, and I thought the book would be published and out by April.

I did meet Darlene when she and Al came to Sioux City in April, but the manuscript was essentially complete by then—or so I thought! I was "taking it to market" to the booksellers fair in Anaheim, California, just as Iowa farmers take their prize pigs to exhibit and sell at the State Fair each summer.

Capt. Haynes was in town to speak at a dinner. While he was speaking, people noticed a lot of Emergency First Responders hurrying into the hall, but didn't think anything about it because these were the people he was talking about in his speech. I, however, was sitting at the table next to the table where they were needed. Those men and women handled the emergency with such finesse that the people at that table and at my table were the only ones in the hall who knew what was going on. On the podium, Capt. Haynes never missed a beat in his speech. He calmly continued as the drama was played out.

An elderly man at the table was having a heart attack. The EMT's quietly lowered him to the floor below the line of vision of the people at the other tables, then encircled him to block the view of what they were doing. They worked and worked and worked on him, but he did not respond. They analyzed the situation, read all the vital signs, discussed it among themselves, and gave up. One EMT, however, would not give up. He worked and worked, long after the other ones had. Finally, he gave up too. It was a sad time for the workers as well as all the guests at the two tables. They moved him to the stretcher . . . then he moved! After only the slightest moment of shocked reaction, they sprung into action again and hurried the man out of the hall. He lived. All the vital signs indicated that he was momentarily dead, but he survived. His elderly wife, however, had a heart attack the next day.

In May, I went to the fair. As it turned out, I found out at the fair that changes had to be made on the book. When I returned to Sioux City, I restricted my activities to my front porch. I wrote from before dawn to after dusk. Two of my neighbors take a walk together at precisely the same time every day. One morning one of the men called out

ED: Oh, you're out in your office again today. Then, pointing to a blooming rose bush in my yard, Somebody put some flowers on your desk. The other man smiled and waved and the dog with them wagged it's tail.

I finished the writing and sent the manuscript in to Carol, my copyeditor. Then, for the first time in about eighteen months, I came out of my isolation and rejoined the world—already in progress. One day in July as I went through the lobby of the post office to pick up mail, I ran into a man I had only met once before. He was reading a notice he had just taken from his box.

BOB: I read here that Darlene Haynes is speaking at the Rotary Club luncheon on Friday. Would you like to go as my guest to hear her speak?

I was delighted. Friday, as I listened to Darlene's speech, I understood what George had been talking about. She was saying the same things I was writing in my book. She, too, was making a plea to people to recognize that there is a secondary trauma that affects the family and friends of the primary victim and to not let them fall between the cracks after the pressure of caring for the primary victim is over. That day, I asked Darlene if I could interview her. She said yes, but we kept missing each other during the time she and Al were in Sioux City.

The manuscript came back and still more changes needed to be made. It took until October before I was able to get the manuscript pulled together enough to be able to feel where to fit Darlene's story in. There was a major problem in interviewing Darlene. I had to find a way to get to Seattle. One day I was hiking with my friend Carolyn.

EMILY: I need to get to Seattle to interview Darlene, but I don't know how I'm going to get there.

CAROLYN: Northwestern Airlines flies there.

EMILY: I know that, Carolyn, but I can't afford to buy a ticket to fly to Seattle on Northwestern Airlines. Carolyn, it takes money to buy a ticket to fly on Northwestern Airlines.

CAROLYN: I've been wondering how I could help you with your project. Now I know. I believe your project is going to help a lot of people who are hurting because it will give them the tools to recognize symptoms of Post Traumatic Stress. I've been saving my frequent flyer mileage to go to Spain. I have two one-way mileage awards that are going to expire before I get enough to go to Spain. I'll just give you those two and you can use them to fly to Seattle and back.

The matter of where I was going to stay in Seattle fell in place next. Some friends who live in the Mid-West had to make a trip to Seattle to put a house on the market for sale. When I had the chance to stay with them, I packed up my office in a tote bag. I put in a notebook computer, portable printer, miles of cables, surge protector, battery charger, lots of paper and off I went. My office was so heavy I could hardly carry it through the airport. But, I put the strap over my shoulder, held my head up high as if there was nothing in it but popcorn and tried to look like a lady. So, this morning I'm in a nearly empty house, up in a little garret room with nothing except a bed and desk my friends moved in and set up for me, a stack of suitcases, and chapters of a manuscript lined up on empty shelves—still writing. I flew in from Sioux City yesterday. (After the week of working in Seattle with Darlene, I had the chance to take the ferryboat to Lopez Island in the San Juan Islands where I wrote until I was tired and slept until I woke, with sporadic meals and walks on the beach in between. By the time I left, I had Darlene's story nestled into the manuscript.)

George, you were right. Darlene's story is an important part of this book. I, on the other hand, was wrong. The book was not published and out by the time you offered to introduce us in April. I'm remembering something Paul Gruchow, my first mentor in writing, told me long ago.

PAUL: Emily, a book is like a baby. It comes when it's ready. (Well Paul, I'm surely having long, hard labor pains with this one!)

EMILY: Darlene, a friend of yours who sat next to you at Al's retirement dinner said you told him a story that night about your emotions after the trauma that needs to go in my book. Can we talk about Al's retirement?

DARLENE: Oh, that was a wonderful time! I've never been on a flight before where I knew everybody in the cockpit and almost everybody on plane. I don't think many people have.

EMILY: Well, maybe political candidates.

DARLENE: Al requested the same flight crew that had flown Flight 232. They were all there physically except one flight attendant who was killed in the crash, but we could all feel that she was there in spirit. Friends, survivors and families booked seats on that flight. One survivor asked to be booked for exactly the same seat he had on Flight 232.

Al's last flight was from Denver to Seattle. We didn't know it, but people in Seattle had planned to give him a water salute and had brought in fire engines. He was to be asked to stop the plane and the fire engines were going to make an arch of water for him to drive home under. It turned out that it had to be canceled because there was an emergency on the plane. A man became extremely sick and needed immediate medical attention. Luckily Gary, the Disaster Emergency Services director from Sioux City and another man who had helped in the rescue of Flight 232 were on the plane and were able to help. Al said over the loud speaker

AL: Well, the Disaster Emergency Services from Siouxland comes to the rescue again.

DARLENE: It was really strange when we stopped and those men in uniform escorted the sick man off the plane. People thought they were police taking him off in custody.

I have family in Denver, so they were all there at the retirement dinner. My cousin Ernie owns Dardano's Italian

Restaurant in Denver. I called and asked him if he could accommodate 150 people.

ERNIE: Don't worry about a thing, Darlene. I'll take care of the menu and all the arrangements. You just bring your friends on over. We'll be ready for them.

DARLENE: And he did. He did a beautiful job. A couple who had been on Flight 232 with their son were musicians. Remember in the movie when they found the guitar on the ground after the crash? That was this man's guitar. They came and he played the guitar.

The crew all came. They made up a poem for Al. I'll go get it and let you read it. (After I read it she said) I'll make a copy for you. That needs to go in your book. (And off she ran to Al's home office and made a copy.)

To Captain Haynes

The left seat in the cockpit of Flight 232
Was occupied by Captain Haynes, a man few people knew.
A modest man of stature, the world would come to see;
For, when asked how he did it, Al said, not "I", but "We"!
From Texas A & M he came, the Navy helped him fly;
United Airlines joined him soon and sent him to the sky.
The times he spent with Little League to help the children grow
Would prove to be an asset when Love would have to glow.
Almost 300 "souls on board"; on board a DC-10

These thoughts would haunt the Captain's mind again and yet again.
And what to do . . . and where to turn . . . The Power had been lost!!!
He turned to Bill and Dudley . . . aware of dreadful cost.
But somewhere in that moment when all seemed like a dream,
As Denny joined the trio, they functioned like a Beam!
Behind the door, the souls on board had all begun to pray;
Some let the tears flow from their eyes while others looked away.
The Captain of the captains in heaven up above
Looked down on Flight 232 surrounding it with Love!
One Hundred Twelve would join Him, the rest allowed to stay;
And He would take the Angel we all knew as Renee!
Sioux City has a cornfield that once served as a bed
To nestle Flight 232, the living and the dead . . .
The cockpit rolled into a ball of wires wrapped with steel
The foursome had now landed; that dream had all been real!
. . . and sometimes today, when Captain Haynes is sitting in a booth calling out high school football plays, remembering his youth.
He thinks of Jan and Donna, of Tim and of Georgeann,

Of Barbara, Jan, and Susan, Renee, and Kathy Shen . . .
He reminisces in the thought that once...there was a day
The Captain of the captains had clearly shown the Way!
Darlene and Danny by his side, Marlene and Tony too;
All watching little Michael . . . as Mike and Laurie do . . .
All looking at the Captain, the one who held the reins
Of blessed Flight 232; the man called Captain Haynes!

From the Crew of Flight 232
Written by Lou Del Castillo

EMILY: The story of the retirement is beautiful, Darlene—so many friends, so much support. But, you were alone the day of the crash during the time after you heard that a plane had gone down on the route Al usually flies, but before you found out whether it was his plane or not, weren't you?

DARLENE: Yes, I had been running around trying to do last minute things for a Little League tournament that Al and I were to be involved in that weekend. I stopped at my daughter's office while I was running errands. She told me a United plane had gone down on that route and told me the number of the flight, but I didn't know what flight Al was on.

I came home and called United Airlines but the line was busy. Then a strange thing began to happen. Friends who didn't even know it was Al's trip started calling or showing up. They just had a feeling they needed to talk to me. Our son came over. Both our sons and our daughter live in Seattle.

EMILY: How did you cope with the stress of not knowing whether it was Al or not?

DARLENE: I don't react to things until I know. I just waited to find out. I don't get all upset until I know what the situation is. Sometimes I think when people get all strung out ahead of time, and then find out it's not true, they can't pull themselves back together again. They've gone to pieces already and they can't recover.

I knew I had to stay calm because I didn't want my kids to go to pieces. They all came to the house immediately. We have two phones in the house. After our children grew up and moved away, we kept the teenage line because we're so involved in Little League activities. We use it for that now.

Both phones were ringing constantly, but we didn't know anything to tell at that time. I wasn't answering the phone, my kids were protecting me from that. We were all quite aware that in an airline crash the cockpit crew seldom survives. Finally, after a couple of hours, an important call came in.

LAURIE: Mom, I think you'll want to take this one.

It was Sister Marlys with the Pastoral Care Staff of the hospital in Sioux City telling me that Al was all right. She gave me a phone number where I could call him. This triggered a family celebration with hugging, kissing, crying and a tremendous sense of gratitude and relief. I immediately called Al. Two plastic surgeons were working on wounds on his head and face, just finishing up plastic surgery, but he could take the call. He was conscious.

AL: I'm all right, Darlene. You don't need to come because I think I'm only going to be here a couple of days.

(One son had strong commitments and could not easily go to Sioux City. The other one immediately said)

DAN: I don't care if he's there one day. I'm going Mom.

I called United Airlines and told them we wanted to leave the next morning. They took care of all the arrangements. They told me we couldn't fly into Sioux City because the airport was still closed, and that all the hotels and motels in the city were taken, so we'd have to take our chances.

I packed, and included a set of clothes for Al to wear home on the plane. I could tell later that I wasn't thinking very clearly at the time because, even though I had just talked to him and knew two plastic surgeons had been working on wounds on his head and face, the shirt I packed was a pullover shirt. Of course his wounds would not allow him to pull a shirt over his head. In Sioux City, I had to go get a button down shirt for him to wear home. Survivors could get clothes if they needed them at J. C. Penny's and not pay for them, so I did.

I sent all the kids, and their kids, home to eat, bathe, and get some rest. It had been a very emotional time and we all needed a break. Then they came back to spend the night with me. We were all together that night, even the ones who weren't going. The next morning my son Dan, daughter Lauri, and I flew to Sioux Falls, South Dakota, an airport 100 miles from Sioux City. United had a representative meet us in Denver where we changed planes. They deboarded us first and hurried us off to the VIP waiting room so we'd have privacy. We were lucky to be able to have privacy that week. We left our house at 5:15 in the morning, and my neighbors told me that at 5:30 two large TV vans with those satellite dishes on top drove up to our house. They wanted to interview me. Because of that mere fifteen minutes, nobody knew what the family looked like.

When we got to Sioux Falls, United had a rented car waiting for us. They had offered to send a driver, but I had told them that my son would drive. We drove south on I-29, the same Interstate highway that the air tower controllers had given my husband as an option for landing the day before.

I knew that there was no room in the inns for us. The media and out-of-town officials had flocked to the scene the day before. I told my son we'd start stopping at the first motels we came to and take our chances. First, we drove into the Holiday Inn and were told, of course, they were booked solid.

CLERK: Wait a minute. I think someone just checked out. Let me check the book—Yes, but the room's not ready yet.

DARLENE: That's okay. We're going to the hospital to visit somebody and we won't be back until late tonight.

I filled out the registration card and when I handed it to her I asked: Please don't put any phone calls through to the room, just take messages. She recognized my name.

CLERK: Yes, Mrs. Haynes, we'll take care of that.

DARLENE: And they did. We were able to walk in and out of the motel while Al was in the hospital and it wasn't until the very last day that one reporter recognized us. My son came back from the bar one night and said people were all talking about us in the bar and trying to figure out where we were. It became our joke with the motel staff.

CLERK: Well, I lost $500 today because of you. People have found out you're staying here, and somebody offered me $500 today if I'd tell them your room number.

DARLENE: After five days, Second Officer Dudley Dvorak, his wife Kay, and our family were flown home in a jet. The men were not well enough to travel commercially. Our first visit to Sioux City was over. It was not to be our last.

Chapter IV

AFTER A TRAUMA THERE MUST BE A CRUSADE TO SAVE RELATIONSHIPS

Trauma changes people. It changes people's lifestyles, their perceptions of life, and their personalities. This is easy to see in the case of a dramatic event that leaves its victim facing life in a wheelchair. Although a new personality and a new value system do not come easily to a person facing life in a wheelchair, it is obvious they must come. It is not as obvious, but just as true, that they must also come in the aftermath of an emotional injury.

The mind must grieve the losses caused by the trauma and journey through the immobilization of thoughts of "Once this has happened, it can happen again. Experience has already proven the unthinkable can happen." Yes, it can; but it probably won't.

The process that provides a vehicle for the journey from devastation of losses of the trauma to the development of a new personality is the grief process. The new personality that develops is grounded in the awareness that "Yes, this could happen again but it probably won't, and if it does, I now know that I am a survivor with the skills to survive again." Trauma is an event; it is not a state of existence. When the event is over, the process of healing can begin. The shock stage is two things at the same time. It is the end of the event and the start of the process of healing.

Grief is a very personal thing, and each person must go through grief at his or her own pace. When two people are committed to support each other through it, it is usually a roller coaster time. Grief is uncomfortable not only for the person going through it but also for the people near. There is often pressure to get it over with and get on with one's life. If either person yields to this pressure and terminates the grief process prematurely, painful molecules of emotion remain stored in the body and can bubble up later to cause problems.

Growth, and new strength, come with survival. However, this very change accounts for a predictable pattern in couples whose lives are affected by trauma. This pattern is often unrecognized while dealing with the overwhelming consequences of the primary trauma. When partners change, relationships change. The two partners are suddenly two different people. Professionals working with emotions of couples after a trauma state that there are almost always two stages: First, there is the shock of a horrible, unexpected catastrophe or perhaps the death of a loved one, and then there is the aftershock—a breakup or a divorce.

Men and women grieve differently. Men in our culture have a tendency to withdraw to heal from a violent crisis. On the other hand, many women seem to be energized by the experience and propelled into action. Women apparently use the positive energy of post traumatic stress to take action to keep others from suffering their fate. If one partner pulls inside during a time of emotional trauma and keeps a wall of silence around feelings, communication is cut off. Each then must go through the process alone.

In the past, little attention has been paid to the victims of secondary trauma from tragedies that happen to someone close to them, for example from sexual violence to their partners. Men suffer from guilt, confusion, and feelings of inadequacy. Sexual violence is a crisis for both the victim and the victim's partner. The process of working through the emotions after a trauma changes both people. When a barrier of silence prevents them from going through the process as a team in a way that allows them to work through their individual pain, understand their partner's pain, and offer each other support, it is common for the changes to lead them in different directions.

A woman's pain in the case of sexual assault is enormous and, without help, the partner may become the scapegoat. Often, women have a hard time afterwards separating the sexual assault from their private sexual lives. Or, the partner may become angry himself. Often, men react to feelings of helplessness with anger. A man may shove his emotions under, deny and avoid his hostility and suffer depression.

When a couple cannot work through their emotions after a trauma, these stored emotions can affect a family years later. Although there are large numbers of couples in trouble, few recognize that their relationships are following a predictable pattern, so few seek help. With help that is available, many of these relationships can be saved.

Nancy and Steven Ziegenmeyer are a couple who were able to work through the emotions and pain together after she was raped in Des Moines, Iowa. Like many women, Nancy put a wall of silence around herself after the assault. But, when Geneva Overholser wrote an editorial in the Des Moines Register about a standard newspaper policy of withholding names of rape victims, she realized that breaking the silence was the only way to take back her life from the terrible grip taboos against speaking out had on it. She and her husband discussed it at length and made a decision as a team. Instead of remaining anonymous, she would contact Ms. Overholser. This resulted in a series of Pulitzer Prize winning stories in the paper which put Nancy in a position of advocate for victims' rights. A book and a made-for-TV movie, "Taking Back My Life", followed. Speaking around the country, Nancy finds a nation ready to stop shaming victims. In the past, sensational rape trials, such as the William Kennedy Smith and Mike Tyson trials, have put a spotlight on the stigma attached to crimes against women. This has kept women silent and in fear of going public. Nancy feels that her speaking out helps women feel less alone and to feel that it is all right to find their voice and use it. She says that women have told her that her speaking out has given them the courage to tell someone. This asking for help is the first step in releasing emotions stored from victimization.

Not all couples are able to work through the issue as a team. Investigator Lois Veronen, a psychologist at the Human Development Center of Winthrop College in Rock Hill, South Carolina, found some interesting things. She found that distress for a couple after a sexual assault is universal and that half of those relationships are destroyed within a year.

Men in our society are socialized to be protectors and controllers but most are powerless in major catastrophes. This inner conflict often keeps them from being able to discuss the event and the trapped anger can turn against the victim. Patience wears thin. There is a need for the victim to be okay, to snap out of it, to put it behind and get on with life as usual. But, life is no longer as usual.

When people live through a tragedy, their identities and personalities change. So do their value systems. It becomes necessary to take a new look at relationships, careers and priorities. Going through counseling together can help a couple examine these things as a team. Differences can be weighed and balanced. Needs can be identified; solutions with value to both can be negotiated. This can not be done in silence. This can only be done by talking about inner pain.

I asked Darlene how she and Al handled this period of transition after the tragedy. I began by asking her about the common period of emotional letdown after the high level of emotional activity dies down—the sort of a baby blues period.

EMILY: Darlene, how did you handle the wind down period after the trauma? Pam and I felt anxiety and confusion and low grade depression. I now know we were going through a form of grieving—grieving not only present events but also emotions triggered in our bodies from events in our past.

DARLENE: I didn't have time for a let-down period. Al's and my life changed drastically—and permanently—because of the crash. We came back to Seattle as different people than we were when we left. We came back to different roles and, more importantly, to different responsibilities. Calls immediately began coming in asking Al to share his experience with groups all over the country. Al had become a public figure.

EMILY: Yes, you temporarily belonged to the public. I experience that same thing as each one of my books comes out. My writing, just like the crash and rescue of Flight 232, triggers strong emotions in people from their past. Al successfully overcame a trauma. He now represents hope to a lot of people.

But Darlene, I don't think that started with the crash. I think it just zoomed to a larger picture with the crash. In doing the research when I was writing *Souls On Board*, it appeared to me that you and Al have always played the role of helping people identify and pursue their happiest potential. I see you two doing the same thing now that you've done for years. The difference is you expressed it through Little League before, you've added speeches and public appearances about overcoming trauma now. You and Al haven't changed. The audience has just widened.

At the time Pam was gathering materials for her Family Reconstruction and I was out pulling rusty barbed wire off old bison fences (probably without even a current tetanus shot), what were you doing?

DARLENE: Al and I have always been very close, and we've always been able to talk to each other about our feelings. When the calls started coming in, we talked a lot about what we should do. We were very involved with Little League tournaments at the time of the crash, so we just continued what we were doing. It was only about ten days after the crash when Al returned to Little League.

Al had been voted Little League Volunteer of the Year for the State of Washington. We went to the game where he was awarded that. All Little League awards are given out at games. Then, he was named Volunteer of the Year for the Western States Region. All the year's voting had been done before the crash. The Western Regional Tournament is held in San Bernadino. Before the game started, they called Al out on the field and told him he was Volunteer of the Year for the Western Region area. That entitled him to go to New York to meet up with the Eastern, Central and Southern area winners. There was a dinner at Mickie Mantle's Restaurant. Then they went to the World Series, the four men were presented, and the winner was announced. I had to come home after the dinner, so I wasn't there to hear the winner announced at the game, but I knew who it was before I left. It wasn't Al.

EMILY: So you really didn't have a let down period after the crash because you were so involved with your life, a very exciting life at that point.

DARLENE: Right. Then, when Little League stopped, Al and the crew began to be invited to go different places to accept awards related to the crash, so we were constantly on the go. Come on. I'll show you the pictures.

As we walked down the hallway where they have the pictures hung, I could feel the presence not only of Darlene and Al, but of the whole crew. As she explained each picture, it was always with "Al and the crew were given this award." "Al and the crew went to this dinner." I saw pictures of Darlene and Al with the President of the United States, a picture of the Duke of Kent handing Al an award, one where the whole crew had gone to Greece to be given an award, etc., etc.

It was very obvious to me that even though she and Al were still very active Seattle Little Leaguers, their league had gotten bigger.

DARLENE: I think the speaking engagements are good for Al and me too. Particularly during the first year or so, I think it was good therapy for us.

EMILY: Yeah. Sounds like you had a "Have Therapy, Will Travel" situation. In order to speak out, publicly or privately, you have to first pull thoughts up into the conscious mind and organize them. Unlike supportive friends, who sometimes tend to protect us, a public audience will let you know immediately if you're not in reality.

Start from the beginning, Darlene. Tell me about your and Al's trip as a team from the shock stage of trauma back to living in reality again. You not only had to adjust to reality again, you had to adjust to a changed reality.

DARLENE: From the very beginning, Al and I had a different perception of the event. When a man or woman assumes the role of captain of an aircraft, he or she is responsible for whatever happens on that flight. Al's been flying a long time, so his mind had many years of being trained that way. So, even during something as tragic and unavoidable as this, his mind accepted full responsibility for it. Al started out with the weight of the total, unshared responsibility that airline captains carry on their shoulders. They are, in fact by rules and regulations written in the manual and also by the emotional acceptance of that responsibility, fully bound to this responsibility.

Al saw the cup half empty. He started out from the point of thinking he had killed 112 people. I, on the other hand, saw the cup half full. I thought he had saved 184. Of course, neither one of us was right. He did the very best he could, but he was not in control of the outcome.

EMILY: Yes, I know. It's like the remark Col. Nielsen made to a reporter. He's the man carrying a small boy to safety in the picture on the cover of the book *Souls On Board*. When a reporter made a remark about his saving the boy he said "I didn't save the boy. God saved the boy. I just carried him."

DARLENE: It was a time when the men had to make some very hard decisions. There were no instructions in the manual for what to do if all hydraulics were lost. The men knew they had to do something but, when they made a decision to act, they had no idea how the plane would react—or even if it would react at all. No one had any previous experience to draw on. No one had even thought that it was possible for a plane to fly with no hydraulics. That's like speeding down a crowded freeway at 70 miles an hour with no power steering and no power brakes—or any other kind of steering or brakes.

In some cases, the men realized that no matter which option they suggested or decided on there would be tragic consequences. They just had to try to pick the lesser of evils.

EMILY: Yeah. The National Transportation Safety Board's *Operations Group Chairman's Factual Report of Investigation* says "the indicated airspeed on the approach was close to 180 knots." That means that plane was coming in at over 200 mph, no brakes, and a river at the end of the runway!

DARLENE: Right after the crash when someone asked him if he had therapy, Al said no. It wasn't until some time later that he began to realize that yes, he had. Both United and the hospital anticipated the reaction a captain would have, and both had professionals working with him from the very beginning. During the time he was trapped in the wreckage of the cockpit, during the ride in the ambulance, and when the doctors were working on his head and face wounds, he was slipping in and out of consciousness. He didn't remember at first, but later he remembered there was a man holding his hand and talking with him. There were two men working with him. They alternated, and one or the other was with him—talking with him—during those days when he was in the hospital. He says he thought at the time they were just talking, but he now realizes how important the work they were doing was.

EMILY: I've heard Al give his speech. I laugh because he says he does not give speeches, he "gives speech"—just one speech in different places. In his speech, he gives you a lot of credit for his recovery. He speaks about the importance of talking to release the stored emotions and says you were the one there for him to talk to. To me, that seems an advantage for him, but one that must have put a tremendous stress on you. It seems you were having to deal with a double burden of coping with the after-emotions of how close you came to losing him plus the secondary sadness of his pain. So many times people stuff the feelings of the secondary trauma because it's just not accepted to stomp your foot and scream "I'm hurting too." Often the pain of the primary victim is just so much more obvious that the secondary victims feel guilty about worrying about their pain. How did you cope with those feelings?

DARLENE: Al and I have always been close, and we've always helped each other through difficult times. I just wanted to help Al, and I decided the best way I could do that was to simply be there for him for him to talk to or not talk to, to share feelings or not share feelings. I helped by being a crutch of trust that, through experience, he has learned will not break and let him down later. He knew I was not there temporarily, but would be there again and again and again.

EMILY: But Darlene, that type of trust has to be there ahead of time. It's like a bank account. You draw out of it what you've deposited ahead of time.

DARLENE: Yes, and we did draw out from it time and time again. Months went by and we thought we had dealt with the emotions and then someone would call to talk and the tears would come again. Then we'd go back and talk it out again.

EMILY: That must have been hard on you. How did you keep doing that? How did you keep from getting drained?

DARLENE: My family was my support group. My family went with me to Sioux City. The psychologists talked to us too those days we were there, so we had been given the tools to work with. The love I was giving Al was not draining me dry because the love my family was giving kept filling me up again.

EMILY: Wow! But Darlene, that's wonderful for people who have connection before a trauma, but what about people who have not built up their bank account before a tragedy happens? Everything we've been saying says to me that in order to get through a trauma you have to build up strength ahead of time. It sounds like if you don't do it, and a crisis comes, you blew it.

DARLENE: I don't know. (We both sat there baffled for a while. Then, her eyes began to twinkle.)

Oh! Now I know! It's like any other bank account. If you don't build up your assets ahead of time and you get in a spot where you have to have money, you just have to find somebody who has . . . and ask to borrow some. Then, after they've helped you and you're stronger, you pay it back to someone who needs help!

Chapter V

WRITE (RIGHT) TO RELIEVE PAIN OF EMOTIONS AFTER A TRAUMA

Darlene was right. There had been a time when my whole world and everything I believed in had come crashing down around me and I had not been able to handle it alone. I needed to find people who had more strength than I did at the moment to help me. There were willing people there. Because I am an author I was taught to journal (to put my feelings down on paper each day) as a way to help release stored emotions.

I turned back to my paper friend, my journal, when Pam left town. She finalized the opportunity at the Air Force Academy, followed her heart, and went to Colorado. She had already done much of her part of the book project that needed to be done in person, and we kept in close contact by phone. When a nearby university press asked me to publish with them, I discussed it with her and agreed. We began to learn the publishing business and found it fascinating.

I threw myself into writing the book. Since my divorce, my writing had been about pain, and this too was about pain. However, now I was writing about other people's pain as well as my own. This new experience extended the boundaries of my self-image. For years I had isolated myself within the walls of my home and had little contact with people. My pen and paper were my companions. Now I had to get out and talk to people, collect photographs, and find artists to do original art work. As the book grew, I grew.

I found that I could not write about other people's pain unless I acknowledged and faced my own pain. Denial and avoidance is not an option for an author if a manuscript is to be nonfiction. Even if a book is based on a real experience, if reality is not written the book is fiction. As I wrote about other people's pain, I found that my writing was like bibliotherapy. Bibliotherapy is a form of Experiential Education in which a person who is hurting shares an experience vicariously by reading about it. Stored emotions from past experiences are triggered and, if the person chooses to face them, can be released.

I was Writing to Relieve long before my brain processed and accepted the fact that I had a Right to Relief from chemicals stored from past training and experiences. It was the vehicle that took me there.

In order to write about pain, I had to break the silence of my opiated feelings and acknowledge that I was hurting. Breaking the silence produced more pain because the War Against Silence is a battle, a mobilization of all available resources to fight for relief of pain from secrets:

> Secrets our brains temporarily
> keep from us by producing
> morphine-like chemicals that
> anesthetize us from feeling more
> pain than we can handle at the
> moment, and Secrets society
> imposes on us by taboos on
> talking about some of the events
> that cause trauma.

Almost everybody has a painful secret in his or her background. Whether it is a true perception or not, if one feels it has to be kept secret it is because of a feeling of shame or fear. Both of these emotions produce chemicals that can harm—or kill—us. It takes courage to break the silence and speak out about secrets. In the short run, silence can be the path of least resistance, but in the long run tensions that are not released accumulate and cause other problems. Yes, speaking out about problems definitely takes courage. As with any other behavior, this behavior, too, causes consequences. Many times, when one speaks truth, people leave. People whose life experiences have trained them to choose denial and avoidance as the way to deal with stress will often leave rather than face the reality of truth.

Often, the step from the shock stage of trauma to speaking out to someone else is too big to be taken in one step. It takes too much courage for people who are not yet aware that they have courage.

Some people go through life and never know they have courage, but courage is a necessary ingredient for a healthy life. Life is changeable, and change is uncomfortable. It takes courage to function outside our comfort zone. As we make our judgments and decisions, we must rely totally on self-image which has been formed by our past experiences. Whether our decision is to try or not depends entirely on what our past experiences have taught us. Have our past relationships with plants, animals, and people around us taught us we can do it? Or, have they taught us we must be dependent on someone else to fill needs out of the range of past experience? The culture I was raised in trained both men and women to be dependent personalities. Because of the division of tasks between men's work and women's work, it taught both men and women that they were dependent on the other sex for 50% of their needs. Men were trained to function in the area of supplying material needs. Women were trained to nurture, the area of the soul.

It took courage to continue writing on *Souls On Board* after I realized that in order to write about other people's pain I had to face and release my own emotions. I had not yet processed the information that I had a right to relief from painful emotions caused by other people's behavior. My past experiences had laid down such a layer of corrosion around my feelings that even though I could understand the information intellectually I could not feel this right on the conscious level. When that awareness first broke above the surface, I could feel it in my body as my stomach gave a lurch. When we are attuned to what our bodies try to tell us, we can sense when new awareness are breaking.

I could write about my pain before I could break the silence and talk about it. New information was making old ways of thinking obsolete, but I was not able to process it because my brain had been imprinted with the old information. The hierarchy system I was raised in, the system which molded my self-esteem, had been grounded in distorted thinking. In a hierarchy system, somebody has to be higher—somebody has to be lower, somebody has to be right—somebody has to be wrong. It is a system based on control rather than cooperation. Being raised in such a system had left me with deep psychological wounds, but I didn't know it. Neither did the people who had molded me. The system had screwed me up because the system was screwed up. The people and institutions that had molded me as a child—family, supportive friends, church, schools, etc.—had merely taught me what they had been taught. The sad part was that what they had been taught was wrong but they didn't know it. Most people are well meaning in their attempts to teach the habits they were taught, habits they truly believe will lay a groundwork for happiness and productivity. Sometimes they do not.

It was not until I begin to see the effects of my own habits repeated in my children that I begin to question them. Because of my opiate system, I had not seen the distorted thinking in my own habits. It is the responsibility of the older generation to pass on the habits that have worked for them to the younger generation. It is the responsibility of the younger generation to examine them for reality—for truth. Writing in a journal is an extremely effective way to examine feelings and beliefs for reality—for truth.

After having to disconnect myself from feelings too painful for me to bear for so many years, eventually I lost connection with all my feelings. I not only lost connection with painful feelings, I lost connection with tender feelings too. This same numbness of tender feelings is often reported by Vietnam Vet victims of Post Traumatic Stress but, for me, this did not come as a change. Because this was the way I always remembered feeling, I did not know that it was not normal. For me, this was the way life was.

Gradually, through journalizing, I learned to scrape the corrosion away and identify my feelings. It was an awkward and difficult task.

How do you feel?

I didn't know. (I was given tools to use.)

Just concentrate on four feelings: Mad, Glad, Sad, and Scared.

I still didn't know. I was taught to pick the closest one by eliminating the others.

Mad? No, I don't think so.

Glad? No.

Sad? Yes, I feel a little sad.

Scared? No, I don't think so.

Still, I wasn't feeling emotions. I was simply analyzing and intellectually picking the closest one. The area of my soul was numb. I was operating totally in the area of my mind. As a child, I was not permitted to show emotions, and physical activity was held to a minimum. I had the traditional skates and bike, but lived with the constant admonition "Be careful. You might hurt yourself." I had never been taught to swim, although I lived a mile from Lake Ponchartrain in New Orleans, because water was dangerous. This caused me problems later on because a requirement for graduation from Louisiana State University was passing a swimming test. With so many bayous in Louisiana, I guess curriculum writers figured it was a necessity.

I couldn't pass the test. I kept trying and trying, but I was too afraid of water. I repeated the course several times. As graduation neared, my friends got very concerned. I can still visualize in my mind the picture of the day I passed my swimming test. When Huey Long was Governor of Louisiana, he was determined to have the biggest and best swimming pool. He built a beautiful one. Someone built a bigger one, so the story is he made his bigger. I can see the seam at the bottom of the pool where the addition was added. In my mind I can see columns supporting a balcony where my friends were standing and cheering me on. I finally passed the test four days before graduation. I practically went down the aisle with cap and gown and wet hair!

With emotional and physical areas closed to me, I had only one area open to me—the intellectual area. Children are survivors. I guess I quickly figured out that as long as I made only the minimum movements (like walking and moving my head and arms slowly and sedately), and kept a deadpan expression on my face, I'd not be admonished. But, I had free reign on the inside. The full range of joys were mine in my thoughts! I could climb the highest mountain, run through the most beautiful meadow of wild flowers, and feel the salty spray of the ocean on my face . . . and I did!

I made up an imaginary friend and named her Shirley, after Shirley Temple. My mother bought me a life-size Shirley Temple paper doll (with changeable clothes) and hung it on my closet door. Shirley was my only friend as a child because real children made too much noise to be invited over to the house. I thought the minister knew about her because I thought he kept saying that Shirley, goodness, and mercy would follow me all the days of my life. She still does. I can actually feel her presence now on the conscious level.

Now, I understand many of the things that happened to me as a child. I now know that when a child is raised in the dysfunction of rigidity to the point of being unhealthy, the different parts of its personality sometimes split off and become separate personalities instead of being integrated parts of the whole. We all have separate personality parts. It's healthy to have different parts because we need them to do different things we need to do. However, in children who come from unhealthy dysfunctional families, these parts can split off from each other. It is a survival mechanism. When they do split off, each fights for control rather than cooperates. When one part is in control, the others have no influence on decisions. We need all the parts to have their say for checks and balances. Otherwise, we make some very distorted decisions and cause a lot of problems. Unfortunately, this all goes on the subliminal level and the person involved doesn't see it. He or she does, however, have to deal with the effects of the consequences of the decisions. So do the people around him or her.

Shirley and I are working on this, and when she feels safe enough to come back and be part of the group, along with the other needed parts of my personality, I'm going to throw a Parts Party.

There'll be plenty of chocolate for Shirley. (Shirley thinks if it isn't chocolate, it isn't dessert.)

There'll be a whole research library of books for the Intellectual Part.

There'll be calculators, adding machines and spread sheets for the Responsible Adult.

There'll be a butte (an isolated mountain with tall straight sides) for the Physical Part to climb.

There'll be supportive people for the Part that is trying to destroy me, the Part that says "Give up" "Take the easy way out". The problem with taking the easy way out is that the enemy often already has the path mined so I'll be destroyed.

There'll be lots of friends for the Part that longs to connect with other people.

And, there'll be music . . . lots and lots of balloons and music!

My journal reminds me of balloons tied to a string, or bubbles blown from a soup bubble ring. I call my journalizing Bubble Babbles because, as each emotion bubbles into my consciousness, I quickly write it down and draw a circle around it. As I see areas of connection, I connect those bubbles with an arrow. Sometimes they look like a bunch of balloons tied with strings. I hold tightly to the strings long enough to put a stop-action camera on in order to examine them and not let them float off out of sight.

I try to take time, relax, and experience the feelings written in the bubbles. I pay attention to what associated feelings bubble to the surface, then draw an arrow out from the original feeling and put each new feeling in it's own circle. In it's own time, I let my mind focus on each feeling as it relates to the feeling in the original circle. I let new feelings bubble to the surface and attach these new circles in a ring around whatever bubble triggered it. Sometimes I reach the edge of the page with the bubble, the attached bubbles' bubbles, and the bubbles' bubbles' bubbles. I simply tape another page on that side and let them keep going. Sometimes I have three, or maybe all four, edges of the original page extended with taped-on pages. Sometimes the taped-on pages have taped-on pages.

There are days when I am full of anxiety and conflict and a flood of emotions fight to be released. My freeform journal takes on weird shapes as I write and write and write. Eventually, one or two primary feelings begin to flow. I can see when I begin to focus in on the real problem. The taped pages begin to extend out in a straight line. When the thoughts stop, I can usually go back and see very clearly what my major points of conflict are. I can then bounce these selected few off a supportive friend in order to run them through a reality check.

One of the problems in trying to release emotions after a trauma is that the process takes longer than we can afford to pay a professional or longer then the attention span of even very close friends. I use my journal as my paper psychiatrist to help me identify my pain and, just as importantly, help me find ways to clearly communicate my feelings to others. When I ask for someone's help after an extended period of babbling on paper, we both can better understand what help I need. I think friends are more willing to help when I help myself first.

Because of our body's ability to block us from seeing the whole picture, we can seldom return to reality alone. We need friends. We need connection. But, we cannot ask other people to do what we need to do for ourselves: experience our own pain.

FRIENDSHIP

What is a friend?
Someone to sigh with,
Someone to cry with,
To be with through smiles and woes,
Someone to talk with,
Someone to walk with
Wherever a path in life goes.
A friend is a treasure,
An all around pleasure
To share with, to care with and love.
Wrapped with affection,
And made to perfection,
A friend is a gift from above!

by Alice Joyce Davidson from her book *Because I Love You,* (c) by Alice Joyce Davidson 1982, and published by Fleming H. Revell, division of Baker Book House,

—given to me by my friend, Toni Gerber.

Chapter VI

ANALYZING OBJECTIVE AND APPROACH

Through my journalizing I could see the effects of an inner self-image transmitting instructions to me from the subconscious level that I had no awareness of on the conscious level. I could see the effects of my self-image long before I understood the process of how it worked. Recently, that piece of the puzzle unexpectedly fell into place. It began on a business trip to California. I wound up having to spend over an hour in a car rental waiting room so I used the time to work on my manuscript. A young agent came over.

AGENT: What are you writing?

EMILY: I'm an author and I'm writing a book on how to help people who are hurting learn how to get relief from emotions after a trauma. I'm having trouble because, even thought I see it happening, I don't understand how it is happening. (He listened for a while as I explained some of the things that had happened to me in the last couple of years.)

AGENT: You're talking about Psycho-Cybernetics. I teach that in my home in my off-time from this job. I use a book by Maxwell Maltz. Read it. It'll clear up your confusion.

I looked and asked in the bookstores while I was there in California, but I couldn't find the book. Two months later, on another trip to California, I visited a friend Carolyn who lives in Laguna Niguel. As my eye wandered across her bookshelf, I saw sitting there the twenty-year-old book. She let me borrow it and I found out that at about the same time scientists were having significant new awareness about the workings in the physical area, (the brain), a doctor was having new awareness about another part of the wheel that must be in balance in order for our lives to run smoothly—the area of the soul (feelings). Dr. Maxwell Maltz was one of the world's most famous plastic surgeons. It was as a result of his work in plastic surgery that his questions—and later his awareness—began. In his book *New Faces—New Futures,* he had described case histories where plastic surgery, and particularly facial plastic surgery, had dramatically changed people's lives. Then, like any author, he found that the answers to questions of the first book didn't put the matter to rest. The answers only spawned more questions! What about his failures? In his work, Dr. Maltz had noticed that some patients' lives dramatically changed after his successful operations. Some people headed down a path of new opportunities and satisfactions. However, he also noticed that some people with equally dramatic physical changes did not.

In the book *Psycho-Cybernetics* Dr. Maltz explains that our body has an automatic, goal-seeking mechanism that will seek the goal our brain assigns it. Since it is simply a servomechanism (a control system) it can only steer us to a goal but can not select a goal. It is like any other servomechanism triggered by mechanical or electrical impulses. It seeks to keep us on the path our brains' neuromessengers assign it to. Our brains work similar to a computer. They, like computers, seek to determine answers by comparing relationships of stored information and combinations of information. Cybernetics is the comparative study of calculating machines and the human nervous system. It pulls the two together. The principles of Cybernetics shed light on the brain and nervous system's complex goal-striving mechanism. It can work for us as a success mechanism, or against us as a failure mechanism, depending on what instructions it gets from our self-image.

Because our self-image was developed by our past experiences, it can be changed by our present experiences.

During the process of being stored, information from experiences in the present scans information stored previously to find its own pigeonhole in the schema of our mind. If it runs into contradictory information, we feel confused. This forces us to run a reality check on both the new and old information. Resolving the contradiction alters perception and self-image.

The mental or spiritual concept a person has of herself or himself is self-image. It reflects an inner connection, or lack of connection, with a spirit of reality—whether it be an unseen spirit of reality within us or reality in the world around us. This connection is the real key to personality and behavior. When self-image changes, so does personality and behavior. Self-image sets the boundaries of a person's accomplishments because it defines what he or she thinks is possible. Awareness gained from new experiences can override a negative self-image molded by past experiences.

My friend Dan and I met when we were appointed to a seven-county board to study ways to coordinate projects in the Loess Hills of Iowa. At almost every meeting he told me we were doing the same thing in our work and asked me to come out to let him show me what he was doing. I saw no similarity between his swinging through the woods on a rope and my intellectual endeavors. Finally, to get him off my back, I went. When I did, I could see how he and Scott, his partner in REAL Adventures, used the principles of psycho-cybernetics. The goal of REAL is to help people get "Real Excited About Learning" through Experiential Education based on adventure.

Dan and Scott believe that people of our society are information rich and experience poor. We are continually flooded with information and theory, but there aren't many opportunities to explore tangible learning experiences. They think that these are experiences that shed the most light on how we perceive ourselves and others. Unlike many people who share these views, they took action on their beliefs. They searched until they found a spot to anchor their belief, a place to make it tangible. They chose a combination wooded and prairie area in the Loess Hills and put their money where their mouths were. They built a Ropes Teams Challenge Course.

The course is made up of wood, rope, and cable settings on the ground and in the trees. Each setting presents a unique challenge for an individual or a group. To me, they looked impossible to do. They are without using a lot of creative thinking and without pulling on past experiences and abilities most of us don't realize we have. Dan and Scott believe that people who make an effort to surpass self-imposed limitations grow in self-confidence and self-awareness.

Gradually, as we discussed our personal beliefs and projects, I began to realize that their Teams Challenge Course and my Write (Right) To Relieve Emotions project were both based on the mind-body-soul wheel of life and were simply two approaches to the same goal. As people progress through the course and become aware that they are actually performing far above their perceived capabilities they are forced to alter their image of their capabilities. A similar thing happens when I teach people to put their feelings in writing in a journal. An experience in the present will help a person understand the past because it dislodges feelings stored from similar experiences in the past. Once dislodged, the feelings must be faced. The problem is that often a feeling can be triggered and felt before the mind recalls the memory. The mind might have the memory opiated and blocked out.

Although feelings may seem disconnected at the time, capturing them on paper creates a tangible record that each person can analyze and reflect on at his or her own pace. Connections that our minds have perceived, whether reality or not, become apparent. As connections are seen, reactions dislodge other feelings. The mind's associations become clearer and patterns and habits become apparent. If the self-image of the present and a dislodged self-image from the past don't mesh, the confusion forces a reality check. The process of resolving the conflict forces other new awareness, an altered self-image, and personal growth.

Because we experience each event at many different levels, the key is the association the mind draws between the three points of the wheel of life. The area of the body receives stimuli from tangible experiences. The hands can hold a rope. The feet can feel a log attached to a tree ten feet up in the air. The body can feel the straps of the safety harness. Writing captures the thoughts that come to mind when a climber looks down from a 14 foot wall just scaled; chemicals express the feelings generated in response.

When I journal, I find that a forward scout bubble comes up to test the climate first. Quickly, I write the feeling down and draw a circle around it. Then, if safe, the message is relayed back and others expose themselves. When writing puts the stop-action camera on a feeling, I can take the time to focus on that one and see if it is just the forward scout for many others still hidden in a security area.

I began Writing to Relieve emotions long before my brain had processed the information that I had a Right to Relief from painful emotions from the past. The rigid culture I was raised in taught me to stuff my emotions, and that it was wrong to be too emotional or to release negative feelings. In my mind I was aware that I now had this right, but my self-image blockaded my acceptance. Journalizing was one of the tools used by people trying to help me make the transition from the shock stage of trauma to the point where I was strong enough to break the silence. I didn't understand the process. My mind was far too anesthetized to process painful reality at the time.

The Write(Right) To Relief method does not require understanding of the process. It works in the area of feelings, not the area of the mind. It guides us to put less focus on thinking *about* a problem and more on experiencing the feeling. Because writing helps us to become aware of our inner feelings, it can lead us to challenge a distorted self-image perception that we have no right to relief from painful emotions. Emotions are stored by experiences; they can be released by experiences.

As Dan and Scott walked with me through the wooded area of the course for the first time, thoughts began to come. I had been raised with a firm concept of climbing the ladder of success and of taking time to go through each step before stepping on to the next rung. The accepted schools, the accepted neighborhoods and the accepted organizations were all important. I now began to think that maybe sometimes one has to go beyond a ladder to a rope. Ladders rest on past experiences. They must rest solidly on a foundation of the known. The movement of change can topple them. Ropes, on the other hand, have the ability to fling out and hook on to future experiences.

When life hands us a rope, we can choose how to use it. A rope can bind and limit, can encircle and confine, or bind and connect, bind and bond. A rope can set boundaries to stay within, or it can be thrown out into the unknown on faith to lasso a future to climb toward. If we choose to climb a rope to a future, we must worry about what's reasonable to worry about and move in faith toward the rest. The key word is move. Our body's servomechanism works on movement. Like a torpedo shooting through water toward a goal, we get off course and make mistakes. Our servomechanism corrects our course and we continue on our way. Like a torpedo, if there is no forward movement, we sink to the bottom. When one climbs a rope, he or she must rise above past experiences. As in the Ropes Challenge Course, each person chooses the level of risk they are willing to accept. I am a risk taker; I am not a gambler. In life, each person must personally decide when risk taking becomes gambling. In addition to the rope I fling out to hook onto the future, I want my mind to pay attention to another set of ropes - intertwined and interwoven into a safety net below me. This safety net is woven of strands of reality.

When I fling my rope into the future to hook on to my potential, I miss my mark many times. I fail. Failure is as much a part of life as success. If I am not failing on a regular basis, I am not growing. I'm simply repeating known experiences. When I move into experiences of the unknown, I don't know how to do them. When I build on new experiences instead of experiences I've learned in the past to be tried and true, I will fail on a regular basis. I will fail, however I can choose ahead of time how far I will fall. At the point I choose, I can put other ropes as a safety net. My stored knowledge and resultant intelligence formed from Past Experiences is my Experiential Education. My experiential education and my emotions must be in balance (and based on reality) for my wheel of life to continue to run smoothly. Accepting responsibility for filling my own needs is one of the ropes in my safety net. Connection is another: Connection with others and with an unseen spiritual base. Honestly about my feelings, (starting first with honesty to myself), is another rope. There must be no denial and avoidance in my safety net.

Later that Sunday afternoon, as the three of us sat relaxing on a hillside among the yucca, the purple flowered iron plant and other prairie flowers, awareness of the commonalty of our beliefs and goals grew. As the length of the conversation grew, the bonds of our friendship grew. We come from backgrounds of dissimilar and diverse experiences and I was surprised how comfortably we were communicating. We had been cooperating on the same goal for a long time, even though we had not known each other. The thought that began to form was surprising to me.

Communication Through Cooperation

I thought, "Is that the way it is supposed to be? Do we in the world have it backwards? Is a vital element in negotiating to get our needs met the need to work together first to build empathy for each others needs?"

There is an example of this in my own life. I do not have a large office building or full-time staff. Instead, I use what I call Satellite Staff, people who can show me a portfolio of their skills (either a tangible portfolio or work they have done in the past that speaks for itself) and are able to do specific tasks I need on a contract basis. It was at a seminar that I learned to recognize, define, and analyze my needs and approach. Just as importantly, I met people there who had compatible needs. A few had needs that were mirror images of my own, and I immediately began working very closely with them. They filled my needs, but needed my talents to fill theirs. As we worked together, our understanding of each other's needs grew. As we understood each other better, we were more capable of, and more interested in, filling each others needs.

In this electronic age, it is no longer necessary for a team to all live in the same town. With computers, modems, faxes, phones and overnight mail, it is only necessary to share talent, not geographical location. Pam lives in the mountains of Colorado, Dan is an author and runs a book publishing and promotion consultant business from his home in Santa Barbara. Barbara (from Santa Barbara) has a Public Relations firm and lives in California. So does editor Carol. The electronic age has now made it possible for people to fit their work into their chosen lifestyle instead of the other way around.

Chapter VII

THERE WAS A CONFLICT BETWEEN MY PUBLIC IMAGE AND SELF-IMAGE

At this point, I entered into a very scary period. The university press had difficulties that slowed all their manuscripts to a standstill. I had some decisions to make and I knew I had to make them on my own. By the time I realized the press' role was questionable, Pam was involved in her new life in Colorado. Because of the timeliness of the topic and the effect a long delay would have on the book, it really boiled down to two choices: let it die or continue the work in progress on my own. Working on the book had moved me from self-imposed isolation to success and enjoyment working with people. Before I wrote for my own satisfaction; now I was writing for publication. My self-image was changing from a woman who was uncomfortable around people to a woman who enjoyed being with others.

I started laying groundwork for continuing the project myself, but I was still unsure of what my decision should be. I figured out exactly how much it would cost to finish the project following the same plan the university press had started. I live with a feeling of a connection to an unseen spirit and, as I often do when I am scared and confused, I asked for a sign. I said "This is the amount it will take to finish this project on my own. If I'm meant to do it, this is the funding I will need."

My gut feeling was that I should continue. One morning I called my stock broker and told him I wanted to draw out the amount of money needed to cover the proposed budget. He told me I could pick up a check that afternoon. Incredibly, by that afternoon I did not need the check. A mistake in my favor had been discovered in my checking account in exactly the amount I had said I needed. I live on an extremely tight budget and couldn't believe such a thing could happen. However, it has proven to be just one of the many pieces of the puzzle that have since weirdly fallen into place exactly when needed—no sooner, no later. I am working on, and having some success with, accepting this and not trying to analyze it. I am learning, through experience, that it is my responsibility to do my best to keep the points of my mind/body/soul wheel in balance, then roll along with my life instead of trying to control it.

Another complication developed. Soon after I started working with the printer the university had been using, it began to have severe financial problems. While the university was still handling the project, the man who had owned and run the printery for twenty-five years sold it to an employee. She was artistic and creative and continued her design and layout work in the same nurturing way she had for years. However, because she had been raised in, and her self-image molded by, a system that taught division of labor tasks into men's work and women's work, she believed money was men's work. Her self-image was of a person who was not capable of handling the financial end. Her husband's self-image, having been molded by the same culture, thought he was. He quit his job in Colorado where he had been working as a construction worker, came home and took over the money management. His work experience until that time had been as a farmer and construction worker. The wife continued managing the creative side. She did not get involved in what was considered the area of men's work. We had great fun working on the project. In hindsight, we can see that we were like three little kids playing a new game on an unfamiliar playground and nobody had the instruction manual.

After the book came out, my life changed dramatically because the public's image of me changed. This caused conflict because my image of myself was still controlled by my brain's channels of thought grooved by past experiences. My self-image was not based on reality but on my perception of reality. Events around the publication date of the book, the one year anniversary of the crash, give a striking example of this.

The day before the anniversary, the Sioux City Journal ran an interesting article about the book. It told about the stories and pictures in the book and about Pam's and my reaction at the time of the crash and the weeks following. That night I was a volunteer helping at the Sioux City Art Center at an unveiling. Three models were being considered in a search for an appropriate memorial to be built in memory of those who died in the crash and those who suffered both physical and emotional injury. Over a hundred survivors, families, and friends returned to Sioux City for a memorial service on the anniversary date. Many of them were at the Art Center that night. As I walked in, the Disaster Services Director, came directly to me.

GARY: Emily, people have been calling me all day asking me where to get your book. Where can they get it?

EMILY: I haven't gotten that far yet. They aren't being sold anywhere. I have them at home. (I was so inexperienced, I hadn't asked bookstores to sell it. There was no place to get it.)

GARY: You have to find a place fast. I don't know what to tell people.

Turning to the manager of the Art Center gift shop:

EMILY: Can you do that here?

MANAGER: I would be excited about that.

GARY: When can I tell them they'll be here?

EMILY: I don't live far; Do you want me to get them?

GARY: Yes.

The manager met me at the curb. I missed the opening part of the ceremony and had to stand up because there weren't any seats. During the ceremony, a woman (I still don't know who it was) came in the dark and asked:

VOICE: Would you be willing to sign books tonight?

EMILY: Yes.

VOICE: We'll have a table up after the ceremony. So when you come out come there.

That ceremony, and the book signing afterwards, was one of the most emotional times in my whole life. I was completely immersed in writing the book for almost a year. As I researched the background of the victims, survivors, friends, families, and Emergency First Responders, I bonded with them. They were my imaginary friends and constant companions.

In order to try to avoid mistakes when I autograph a book, I ask the person's name and write it on a piece of paper first. As I wrote each name, I remembered the person's story, and felt their pain. As I looked up and we made eye contact, my imaginary friend became real. I had never seen many of these people. I just knew them from my research, but I knew them intimately. As I made a comment about the wife someone had lost, or an injury I knew some lady had suffered, the night became more and more emotional for me. Many times, when I made eye contact with someone, our eyes were filled with tears.

This went on, . . . and on, . . . and on, and when the last book was signed, I was drained. Then I was attacked:

OPENING VOLLEY: How many times do you intend to do this?

WOMAN: This commercialism.

I stood there and was pounded with wave after wave of verbal attack. I was so shocked I couldn't even return a volley. This was the woman who had sent out the call asking people to volunteer to help that night—the woman who had asked me to come and help! The public attack took place in front of out-of-town survivors and families. Later after this same woman was quoted in the paper challenging the people who didn't like the model that was picked to do what they had done—raise money and build their own memorial—some donors did just that. Many withdrew their donations, formed a different committee, and chose a design felt to be more in keeping with the compassion the community had felt that day. A bronze statue of the picture of an emergency first responder carrying a small survivor to safety was selected because so many of the townspeople had expressed, both verbally and in writing, that they felt it best expressed the important part of the event, the interdependence of humanity. I thought the same thing a year before, and this was the picture I chose for the cover of my book *Souls On Board: Responses to the United Flight 232 Tragedy.*

After she had spewed out her venom and left, I still stood there in numbed silence.

GIFT SHOP MANAGER: I saw what happened, and I could feel what was happening inside of you. You have just spent hours listening to person after person telling you how much they appreciate your work and one person criticize you. Yet, the negative one is the only one you can feel now.

He was right. I know now, though I didn't then, that was the only one that connected with my self-image. Because my brain had been imprinted during my childhood to see myself as a person who couldn't do anything right, her attack affirmed my self-image. The remarks two hours before rolled off like water off a duck's back. I now realize I became ashamed of my book.

The next morning another incident happened that deepened my feeling of shame. One hospital called and ordered enough books to give one to every survivor who had been a patient in their hospital expected to attend their Open House that day. I called the other hospital and asked them if they wanted any books. Their Chief Executive Officer had been involved with the event where the attack took place and I was told they didn't want to get involved in commercialism. I could feel my stomach react to the criticism although I had felt no reaction to the other hospital's approval. It would be two years before I would be aware of what was happening to the chemicals inside my body and how they were affecting my moods. In the meantime, what I felt would be shame and guilt for writing the book—even as it gained national, and international, attention.

Once the bookstores found out where the books were, they starting calling me to place orders. B. Dalton and Waldenbooks were not allowed to buy from individuals, so they had a distributor call me. I knew nothing about what commission I was supposed to give bookstores, wholesalers or distributors. I didn't even know about the distribution chain.

On a three-way conference call with a chain bookstore and their distributor, I admitted it and asked for advice.

DISTRIBUTOR: Well, my first advice is that you have your book priced too low. You will not be able to pay percentages to all the people who need percentages and be able to continue in business at that price. I suggest you adjust it to a more appropriate price. I'll explain each layer and what percentage each layer has to get in order to survive. (He was very detailed. Later, I found out that what he said was true, and that the verbal agreement I made on the phone was the accepted industry percentages. I was lucky.)

Pam was at my house because she had come back to Sioux City for the memorial service. We loaded boxes of books in our cars and started delivering them to the hospital that had asked for them and to bookstores. It was pouring down rain.

By this time our story had hit the national news services, so calls were coming in. We got a call from an out-of-town radio station asking us to do a radio interview. It was to be Pam, me, the host and Gary, the Disaster Services Director. Neither Pam nor I had ever done that before, or even knew how it was done. We were surprised to find that we didn't have to all be in the same room at the radio station to do a radio interview. All we had to do was be at a telephone no matter what state, or even what country, the telephone was in. Because of the open plan of my home, we could see each other even though we were two rooms apart. She sat in the front living room, I sat in my office in the back of the house, Gary was across town and the host was in another state. It came across the air sounding like we were all in the same room. Pam and I were amazed.

It was our first radio interview experience, and it was a hard one for Pam. Although her voice did not betray her on the air, it hit her like an emotional bombshell when the host asked:

HOST: In triage, how did it feel to be the one to choose who was treated first when time was a matter of life or death?

PAM: I didn't choose who would be treated first. I chose what wound needed to be treated first. Medical triage is the process of classifying or reclassifying the sick and injured according to the urgency of treatment required and type of condition. It's purpose is to use resources most effectively.

This wasn't the only attack Pam had to weather. Many people in town attacked her for being featured in the book when there were so many other people out there too. She didn't do that, I did. A storyline has to focus on a representative character. But, I also made it very clear in the book that many people were doing incredible work that day. That was a day of a Thousand Heroes, not just Pam. She finally got relief when the movie *Crash Landing: The Rescue of Flight 232* was made. People started attacking the man featured in that script instead.

By the time we finished the radio interview, it was time to go out to the airport for the memorial service being held at 4 p.m., which had been the time of the crash. We piled into her jeep but were held up at the intersection at my house because of an ambulance passing. It was going very slowly. Because Pam is trained to recognize signs of emergency response, she knew that there is only one reason why an ambulance would be driving that slowly: respect for the dead. We could both feel the connection with the situation. It was a definite presence, but we could not identify it. We felt it individually: we felt it strongly. It was not until later that we understood. A few blocks away, our friend's son had drowned in the runoff of the downpour of rain as it rushed past the curb in front of his house.

Darlene Haynes was back in Sioux City too.

DARLENE: That day, Al and I spent two hours at each one of the hospitals' Open Houses. It was an emotional time. It seemed very important to people to know that Al was all right. The thing that struck me most was that they not only wanted to talk to him, people seemed to be compelled to *touch* him. Time after time, people would reach out and physically touch us both. They'd touch our arms, or shoulders, our backs. It was as if they had to touch us to know that we were okay.

A couple of doctors told us later that they stood in the hall and watched people as they went in and out. They said you could see the difference on their faces after they'd been in. They said the faces were strained and anxious going in. When they came out, they were relaxed and seemed at peace with the situation. It was eerie. I felt the whole memorial period was therapeutic. That's happened again and again. We think the situation is closed, then something will happen and the emotions flood back again.

EMILY: Yes, I know. Post Traumatic Stress is like a boil. The covering is lanced by something that happens in the present and a little of the pus oozes out. Sometimes you think it is all out and that the healing is finished. Then, unexpectedly, something else will happen and the pain starts oozing out again. It doesn't all come out at one time, but each time it is lanced the pressure is reduced. The threat is, of course, that when the level gets down to where it is not unbearable, people will stop working on the problem. Even though it is a lower level of pain, people who do that still live with unnecessary, and often unidentified, underlying pain.

Pam and I and Darlene went out to the airport from our different locations. Because of the downpour, everyone assumed that the Moment of Silence/Fly Over Missing Man Formation by the 185th Tactical Fighter Group, Iowa Air National Guard scheduled during the memorial service would have to be canceled. We couldn't see the sky anyway. At the very time the planes were scheduled to take off, however, the clouds broke and visibility returned. The planes flew over. Everybody in the airplane hanger where the service had been moved seemed to be affected by the drama of this coincidence. People in the airport hanger were also affected by another awareness—the contrast between the weather that day and what it had been a year before. July 19, 1989, had been a beautiful, sunny day with clear visibility and ground that was not soggy and muddy. If there had been a raging storm, as this July 19, there would have been little likelihood that any of the survivors sitting in the hanger would have been there. "Five Minutes to Live", excerpts from a sermon by Rabbi Kenneth Berger was read. Rabbi Berger was a victim killed in the crash.

After the service, people milled around and there were poignant reunions—reunions between patients and caregivers, some of whom had to introduce themselves. Many patients had been so severely wounded they had been unrecognizable at the time. There were reunions between media people and survivors they had interviewed a year ago—reunions between people who had worked at the crash site—initial meetings between people who had worked in the morgue, had read about survivors but had never seen them in person. These people had only seen the tragic side of the tragedy. One survivor said "That's why I came back to Sioux City today, so that people who helped me could see that I'm okay now."

Captain Haynes was one of the speakers at the memorial service but Pam and I didn't go up to speak to him afterwards because, by this time, I was living with shame for having written the book because of two critical remarks. It was not reality. Every other comment had been supportive.

One of the things I quickly realized after the book was published was that university presses have little need, or money in their proposed budgets, for promotion. Sales are to instructors and students. I had no money written in my budget for promotion, nor any idea what to do to promote a book if I had had money. When I found out it costs as much to promote a book as to write, edit, design, lay out and print it, I was shocked.

One day, when I was on the verge of giving up, I got a promotional letter in the mail from a man who seemed to know about such things. "Since you have just applied for your first ISBN number, I thought you might not know much about book publishing and promotion. Here is information on what services I can offer you." It was from Dan Poynter, a book publishing and promotion consultant, and author of *The Self-Publishing Manual.* International Standard Book Numbers are printed on book covers. They are like a book's Social Security number. People use them to identify a particular book when they want to order it. I read his brochure and was impressed but I had no money for promotion. My friend Carolyn got excited.

CAROLYN: Emily, I have what I call my "God Fund." It's money I set aside for projects I think God wants done. I think your book is one of those projects because it will help people recognize and overcome pain caused by emotions. I think we should go to California and attend this Dan man's seminar. We can share a room to reduce your expenses. If you need to, we'll take money from the God Fund.

Carolyn had been supportive of this project from the very beginning. I suddenly realized that it could never have gotten as far as it already had without the role she had been playing. Without her, the project could have folded at several points.

Case in Point: When I was married I did not drive in the snow. In fact, I seldom went out in the snow without my husband. Snow was definitely men's work. Iowa is snowy country and, after my divorce, I had two choices. I could stay snow-bound all winter or I could learn to overcome my male dependency in this area and learn how to function in the snow. I decided to try—and I had a ball trying. I started tagging along on our county naturalist's public outings. Dawn taught me to hike through the woods in the snow. I even took cross country ski clinic lessons from her. The winter went well and I thought I had mastered Iowa winters. Wrong! I didn't realize that mastering snow was different from mastering ice. The next winter I slipped on an icy sidewalk just outside my back door and broke my shoulder.

This happened the day after I had written the very last word and completed the manuscript for *Souls On Board*. Carolyn came over, and packaged up four manuscripts. She mailed them to people who had agreed to read them and possibly write comments to go on the cover of the book. Then she took me shopping for my new, more appropriate wardrobe—at Goodwill Industries. We bought men's shirts large enough to fit over the immobilized arm which now had to be strapped to my chest, and slacks with elastic waists that could be pulled on with one arm. She even bathed me at first.

I was working for the 1990 Census at the time. Working for money was a very hard thing for me to do. After my divorce I needed to earn a living, but I kept sabotaging myself. I now know that it was because of a very powerful subliminal message that was controlling me without my realizing it. It was a secret from me. The secret message that was controlling my life was finally uncovered in therapy. My culture had trained me with the association of "Women who work for wages are sluts." Men controlled the jobs for which money was paid and my culture had imprinted on my brain that the only thing a woman had to contribute was sex. Extending that, it had also taught me that women who swapped talents and abilities for food and shelter by means of money rather than a gold wedding ring were sluts.

I was aware of none of this on the conscious level. I just knew that after my divorce I desperately needed an income, but when I got close to landing a job, I repeatedly avoided it or sabotaged myself. I think my brain figured the 1990 Census wasn't a "real" job. It would only be for six months, working with friends I socialized with, so I tried. That experience proved to be a major turning point in my life. I was still being bombarded with subliminal messages, but the messages my senses were picking up in the present were just the opposite. This caused me a great deal of anxiety, anxiety I thought was a reaction to the current situation. I now know it was due to my reaction to emotions triggered from a situation in my past. I never would have found relief from the pain as long as I focused on the present situation. The root of my anxiety was a distorted perception of reality from the past. I subconsciously believed, because I had been taught by experiences of my culture in the past, that women who work for wages are sluts. But, my experience in the present as I watched the women who worked at the Census Bureau was: Women Who Work For Wages Are Terrific!

Granted, it was a unique group of men and women making up that particular office staff, but that's not the point. The point is my experience was teaching me that some, even if not all, woman who work for wages are NOT sluts.

The subliminal conflict between these two experiential teachings was what was causing my anxiety. I recently talked with one of the women about it.

EMILY: Nan, one of the first experiences I remember about working at the Census Bureau was your cheerfulness and compassion. I was so upset when I came in for that interview. I know now, though I didn't then, that it was because I felt on the subconscious level that I was compromising my morals.

NAN: Yes, I could see on your face and by your body language that this was a hard thing for you to do.

EMILY: The first days after I was hired were so hard.

NAN: I know. I'd see you sitting all alone at coffee breaks, not talking to anybody.

EMILY: I was watching you. I didn't know you were watching me too. I'd put a chair way across the room from you, but in a spot where I could see you. There were only ten of us working there at the time, though I think it later grew to be about 900 when the Census was in full swing. It was a period when the office and the six-county organization was just being set up. You were always smiling and always helpful. Everybody loved you. You were able to get people to work together who never in this world would have cooperated with each other otherwise. Your desk was right at the front door. Because of security reasons and confidentiality of the information we were collecting on the forms, the door had to be locked at all times.

NAN: I knew everybody who came in. I unlocked the door for them.

EMILY: And you always called us by our first names.

As I was sitting on my isolated chair, watching Nan, a strange thing started to happen. Similarities in this experience in the present began to trigger memories of an experience in my past that I had totally blocked out. The similarity that turned out to be the key that opened the door so my memories could come through eventually became obvious. At first, the memories came through fragmented. But, they kept coming until enough pieces fitted together for the picture to begin to take form.

I was the tenth person employed in this office of the 1990 Census. We were a skeleton team putting together a project that would later be fleshed out with many employees. The spaces were empty now, but later they would be full to capacity . . . and even to overflowing. I began to have a deja vu feeling—a feeling of "I've been through this before." I didn't know when or where. Gradually, as experiences from my past repeated themselves, I remembered when. I began to have flashbacks of experiences from over 25 years before, experiences I had completely forgotten.

Boeing Aircraft Company had gotten the government contract to build the first stage booster for the Saturn V rocket. They set up the facility to build it in New Orleans, Louisiana. I was raised in New Orleans and was back living there temporarily. There had been a series of major disappointments in my life at that time and I had moved back to my home town:

Retreat and Regroup! I got a job with the skeleton crew that Boeing had sent from Seattle to set up the entire operation. Temporarily housed in a huge empty warehouse, the amenities were not much more than desks, chairs and file cabinets.

I felt the same embarrassment, even guilt, about being a female having to "work for wages" though I had not identified the association yet. The problem was the same, the feelings it generated were the same, the fact that my mind was able to mask the association of "women who work for wages are sluts" was the same. As the experiences in the present matched the experience of the growth of the organization, the flashbacks, and guilt feelings, matched them step by step. However, the difference this time was the old belief system simply did not mesh with my experience in the present. The reality of the present experience eventually won the battle and turned my life around. From that experience forward, my life headed down a different path, a path I'd never traveled before: Pride in women in the work force. I had been thinking, and saying in job interviews, that I had no work experience. As the idea of being a woman working for wages became more comfortable to think about, the memory of several jobs I had held began to emerge.

Since I was a computer operator, I figured I'd lose my job when I broke my arm. That didn't happen. Instead of firing me, they moved me to the Public Relations office. My friends, including both new friends at the Census and my old friends, rallied around and helped me do things that made it possible for me to keep my job. Bill, the director, led the campaign. I found that the 1990 Census was where I learned I counted!

Bill and Carolyn took turns with other friends shopping and delivering groceries for me. Because I couldn't drive, Carolyn drove me to the town 100 miles away the day I had to make the critical decision whether to continue with the printery the university press had started with. Together with the new owners, we sat in an old World War II Quonset hut surrounded by the smell of printer's ink and fresh paper to pick out style of print, paper stock, make decisions on layout and design, and select the binding. Later, on one of her visits home from Colorado, Pam drove me up to the printery and helped me make the next round of crucial decisions. It was Carolyn, however, who drove me up the day we turned in all the photographs, art work and the manuscript in its final form.

Afterwards, we went to the small town's city park and ate a picnic lunch we'd brought. Because she suffers from digestive disorders, she is severely restricted in what she can eat. This makes it hard to eat in restaurants. After we ate, we played on the swings. As I looked at her white hair flying in the wind I thought "It's never to late to have a happy childhood."

That day, too, was a day of disaster for Sioux City. As is my pattern, I was up working on the book at 4 am, identifying pictures and putting numbers on them to show their proper location in the book. A terrible rainstorm was raging outside, and I could hear the sounds of emergency sirens. As I worked with pictures of the emergency first responders of the County Disaster Service, I could tell they had been called out to respond to another disaster, but didn't know what it was.

Later, when I knew it was late enough for Carolyn to be up, I called her. She knew what it was. It was a flood, and the creek that runs along the boundary of her beautiful lawn was rising towards her house. It had already risen the length of a football field and had but half a length of one to go before it reached her house. I naturally thought this would not be a day she would want to be driving me across the countryside. But, by the time we had planned to go, she and her neighbor had decided the water wasn't coming any further, and in fact was receding.

CAROLYN: Emily, if it floods it floods. I'd have to evacuate anyway so I'd rather spend the day having some fun doing what we've planned than sitting evacuated someplace.

We went, but we didn't play in the park that day. As we turned the corner on her street when we came home, I could see piles of flooded out furniture in front of every house. My stomach lurched. As it turned out, it had flooded every house north of hers, but had stopped just before hers. I recently went back and asked her to talk about her feelings that day.

CAROLYN: I don't think I felt anything. I do remember that during the night I had been hearing about the flood and I kept telling myself "That's not going to affect me. I have this very deep yard and it's not going to come up enough to bother me." I think that might be called . . . what's the word?

EMILY: Denial.

CAROLYN: (laughing) I think that might come in there. I remember telling myself that that's not going to have anything to do with me, but I'm aware that when I got up the next morning about six, I was a little bit afraid to open the curtains. When I looked out the water was up to my red shed there. I don't know how many feet that is . . . probably a football field.

EMILY: . . .not that far. That's not even half a field.

CAROLYN: I don't know how long a football field is.

EMILY: A hundred yards. Don't you know about it's good to sit on the fifty yard line?

CAROLYN: Yeah. I remember standing there at the window wondering if it was still coming up or not. I went out and the next door neighbor was out too.

NEIGHBOR: Carolyn, it's already going down. See, it's already been up here and it's on its way down.

CAROLYN: So I thought "Well, I missed that." I do remember thinking that if my husband had still been alive he would never have bought a house on a creek anyway. I remember feeling guilty about what he would have thought about my buying one with money he'd earned. I was scared enough that the next day I called and took out flood insurance.

EMILY: You hadn't even taken out flood insurance? A little bit of denial and avoidance there too, huh?

CAROLYN: Right now I'm considering canceling it.

EMILY: What was your feeling when we drove up and saw all those piles of furniture and rugs and things in front of your neighbors' houses?

CAROLYN: I didn't expect it to be my stuff. Maybe I live in denial until something happens. I'm not a worrier. I'll deal with it when it happens.

EMILY: I'm wondering—is it denial or is it faith? In that case I definitely suspect denial, but talk about it as a rule.

CAROLYN: I really don't know. I think a lot of it is faith—not a faith like nothing's going to happen to me, or that because I believe in God he won't let anything happen to me. That's not what it is. Things happen, I don't care how much faith you have. It may be a faith in the sense that the reason I don't worry about things very much is I know that with the help of a higher power, which I choose to call God, I can handle whatever comes up. If I can't stop something, then I usually am able to let it go and think "I'll take care of whatever happens when it happens." Other people call that denial. I don't think they believe me when I say I don't excessively worry about things. I do the best I can and deal with life when it happens.

EMILY: Carolyn, I believe courage is faith, faith that you will be able to deal with things and handle them no matter what happens. I think your self-image keeps you from getting immobilized with fear ahead of time. I know you are aware that bad things happen.

CAROLYN: . . . and can happen to me

EMILY: . . . and have happened to you

CAROLYN: Yeah, I guess so. A lot of bad things have happened to me haven't they?

EMILY: . . . but also that you are a survivor. I think one must almost have to have a connection with an unseen spirit to have the faith to have courage.

CAROLYN: Another thing I see flowing from your idea of the triad of truth, productivity and connection with an unseen spirit is connection with other people. In order to feel that I can deal with whatever happens when it happens, it is imperative that I connect with other people. It is not just me and the unseen spirit that handles something. That, to me, would be more like I am doing things all by myself. I've been that way in the past. I isolated and thought "I don't need other people. I can handle anything with God's help. God and I don't need other people." I have since learned how much I need other people to help me handle anything that happens. I need people to talk to and to encourage me. I need people to support me.

EMILY: . . . and give you feedback when you're in denial

CAROLYN: Yeah. By talking and bouncing things off people I stay more within reasonable bounds of reality and what I need to be doing about something—or not doing about something. It just helps keep my thinking straight. Unfortunately, that includes if they say "Well, Carolyn, I don't know about that. You're in a little bit of denial there." Of course, I don't ever think I'm REALLY in denial.

EMILY: You deny that one, huh?

Soon Carolyn and I started planning our new adventure—a trip to California. Dan only had one spot open for his seminar but when he heard the story he said we both could come. That proved to be no problem because Carolyn didn't get to go anyway. Her stomach acted up and she got too sick to make the trip. I went alone. Although it turned out that we didn't need to take money out of the "God Fund", Carolyn's offer was a pivotal point because it was the catalyst that made the trip happen. I wouldn't even have considered going if I hadn't known I had that safety net to fall back on if I needed it.

Chapter VIII

I REACHED A POINT WHERE I SAW VICTORY IN SIGHT

After the book came out, the experience of being treated like a capable and successful woman conflicted with my previous experiences. I was raised in an environment where criticism and degrading were the methods of training. As conflicting self-images struggled to adjust, I lived with an underlying feeling of anxiety.

Carolyn got sick at the last minute and couldn't go to the seminar in California. I went alone. From the very first leg of the flight I realized how different my life was going to be from now on. I was uneasy not knowing what the public reaction to my book would be, and particularly uneasy about what the reaction of people in the aviation field would be. This was my first airline trip after the book came out and it was, to say the least, uncomfortable. Although I was flying on United Airlines and I knew they knew who I was and knew about my book, I got no clue until the end of the first leg of the trip.

As we were beginning the descent into the Denver airport where I was to change planes, I saw the huddle among the flight attendants but I didn't think anything about it. Then, one of the flight attendants came down the aisle and, as he handed me a bottle of wine wrapped in a crisply starched white napkin, said "With the compliments of the pilots and the crew". I cried. I still have it, sitting proudly on the bookcase in my writing room. Sometimes, on days when the words won't come, I look at it. Often, I cry again.

This was my first experience at being treated like a celebrity as a result of my own productivity. Having been the wife of a music conductor in Washington, DC, I had been exposed to celebrity treatment before, but only as an extension of him, not in my own right. I was so obviously shocked that people on the plane started laughing. When I walked up the aisle to leave, the pilots came out to meet me and the flight attendants hugged me. I loved it!

At the seminar, held at Dan's home high on a hill with a gorgeous view overlooking the Pacific Ocean, we all were treated as if we were special. The weekend was informative, fast-paced and, when we thought we had used every ounce of energy we had, he hiked us down the hill and up again. I not only learned how to promote a book, I met people there with the talent and experience to help me do it. When I came home, I did not feel alone any more.

On the flight home, the pampering continued. When the beverage cart came down the aisle before the meal, one flight attendant told another in a voice loud enough for the passengers to hear "Anything that lady at the window orders is compliments of the crew." After the meal was served and things slowed down a bit, one of the flight attendants asked if she could sit with me a few minutes. She took my hand and talked of her afteremotions lingering from an airline crisis during which she had been in charge of helping passengers remain calm.

FLIGHT ATTENDANT: Most people, including many executives of airlines, don't seem to understand these feelings. What you've written in *Souls On Board* is helping people become aware of the problem. Keep talking to people about it. It helps. Your book explains things pilots and crew feel that I don't think people who have not been through an airline crisis understand. Thank you for writing it.

In Denver, when it was time to board the plane for the last leg of the trip, I thought I was in Japan. It seemed like everybody in the waiting room was Japanese. Well, not everybody was, but there were more who were than there were seats on the plane. A Japanese university had merged with a university near our town. Because this was the airline's first time with so many students flying into our town, they were caught off guard. I was voluntarily bumped and given a round trip ticket in return.

When I got home, I started putting plans I had learned into action. Two weeks later, a call came for an order from the bookstore at the Crystal Cathedral in Orange County, California. The caller mentioned he would like to have me come out. Because of my free ticket (and only because of my free ticket) I could afford to fly out there—which is what celebrity authors do. I was beginning to get the hang of it.

A couple of hours later Barbara called to tell me she was planning to present my project to a group of Emergency First Responders holding a three day session in Santa Barbara. She wanted a supply of books. The training was elaborately staged, complete with a simulated crash of a mock, break-apart plane. Although on the inside I still felt like a little girl pretending to be an author, I was learning to act on the outside as if I actually were a real author—the old "pretend as if" routine. This was probably the first time in my life I had a ticket other than a rock bottom non-changeable ticket. Because it was one I could change, I offered

EMILY: Would it be helpful if I were there in person? I'm flying out Friday to the Crystal Cathedral. Would you like me to see if I can get my ticket changed and come by Santa Barbara on Thursday?

BARBARA: WOW! Would I! That's the sort of thing publicists' dreams are made of.

So, Wednesday I changed my reservation; Thursday I flew to Los Angeles where she had me picked up and driven to

Santa Barbara; and, after flying and being in and out of airports all day, held a press conference at the airport!

There had been a mistake in the first printing of the dust jackets for the books, so a new set of dust jackets to go on the books I was bringing had been mailed directly to Barbara. We hurried to her office, swapped the covers as fast as we could, then went to hand them out to important people.

Afterwards, when we went back to her office, we discovered that the printer had printed the new covers with the softcover price bar code on the hardcover book. That humbled me in a hurry. So much for my credibility. It went down the tube. So much for my new hope of being able to see myself as a capable woman. My old self-image of "you can't do anything right" completely took control. Although the mistake was not mine, my self-image assumed the blame because that was what meshed with what I had been trained to do in childhood. It took me a long time to dig out of that mistake with people in the industry, and even longer to dig out of it with my self-image.

Because I have a passion for trains, I chose to ride the train from Santa Barbara to Orange County the next morning. On the train I met an interesting lady. She and her husband have a graphics company in Burbank. As I was struggling to try to get my suitcase up on the rack above my seat, Patti came across the aisle to help me.

PATTI: What in the world do you have in that suitcase?

EMILY: Books I'm taking to a bookstore. I'm an author.

PATTI: Can I see one?

We dug one out and started our friendship.

Because Marguerite and Ike Eichelberger, my hosts at the Crystal Cathedral, are people who have always been safe people for me, I had a chance to drop back and regroup after the emotional wounds and embarrassment following the press conference in Santa Barbara. I had met Marguerite and Ike on another adventure when they were Tour Escorts on a trip thirty of us took to Korea, Mainland China and Hong Kong. It was the type of trip where the group bonded and the ties remain strong. The morning after I arrived in Southern California as Ike and I were walking to the bookstore, carrying a load of books, an astonished look came across his face and he explained "That's Bob Bragg!"

Okay, I thought, so that's Bob Bragg. I didn't know who Bob Bragg was (that he was currently a United Airlines pilot flying 747s) nor did Ike tell me. He simply introduced us by name. We chatted awhile, then continued on our ways. When we reached the bookstore, Ike introduced me to the manager and gave him the books. Then he said "Give me one of those books back. Bob Bragg's going to buy it."

We retraced our steps to the Visitors Center where Ike knew Bob had been headed. Handing Bob the book, Ike said "Emily's written this book. I think you two have a lot to talk about" and disappeared from sight. Bob was just getting ready to lead a tour of the campus, so I tagged along. After he was finished we talked . . . and talked . . . and talked. I found out that Bob was a pilot of, and survivor of, the worst airline crash in the history of aviation. Two jumbo jets had hit head-on in Tenerife in the Canary Islands. We talked every available minute that neither of us had prior commitments for the week I was there. Mostly, we talked about the afteremotions of airplane crashes.

Talking with airline survivors wasn't new for me. Since the publication of *Souls On Board* I had many such conversations. Just two weeks prior, I had walked into a meeting, located the only available empty chair in the room and sat down—right next to a woman who was familiar with my book and who, like Bob, had also had to jump from a burning airplane in order to save her life. Although the plane had not left the ground yet, a problem with a tire caused it to crash and burn. The escape chutes went up in flames, leaving passengers no chance to escape except to jump.

Later, when I started writing this book, Bob was one of the first people I asked permission to interview to use his story.

SUNDAY AFTERNOON, MARCH 27, 1977: The day had already had its problems for Second Officer Bob Bragg, sitting in the cockpit of a B-747 Pam Am charter flight from California to Las Palmas, Canary Islands. It had been diverted from its original destination because of a terrorist bomb explosion in the airport at Las Palmas so set down on Tenerife, a nearby island. After a three hour delay, things seemed to be okay again at Las Palmas. The planeload of tourists, on their way to a cruise ship, reboarded to resume their trip. The weather was perfectly clear as the three-member cockpit crew taxied the plane out. Suddenly, a fog bank rolled in and completely obscured the runway. Within a few minutes, visibility went from unlimited to 1500 feet. Then there was a break in the fog and, through the windshield, Bob saw a KLM Jumbo Jet coming straight at him. The Pan Am crew frantically began trying to get their plane out of the way, and were actually able to get it turned about 20 degrees to the left. Just before impact, Bob closed his eyes and ducked his head. He was terrified. The KLM jumbo jet sliced off the top of the Pan Am jet but, because of the 20 degree angle, missed the cockpit and the three men in it. Of the twelve flight attendants on board, eight were killed. Bob recalls that within 30 seconds or so he ran the full gamut of emotions: the moment he closed his eyes and ducked his head was the most terrifying moment of his life; the moment he opened his eyes again was the happiest because he realized he was still alive and in one piece. In the worst disaster in airline history, 321 people were killed in the aircraft he was in; 285 in the KLM; 606 total.

Bob knew that if there were any survivors they would have to be evacuated immediately as the plane was carrying a load of fuel and would soon explode. With two choices of escape route—through the cabin or out the cockpit window onto the fuel-filled wing—he chose to jump over the shattered window. He then began evacuating passengers onto the wing. Once they were there, he had to encourage them to jump 40 feet to the ground as that was their only chance of survival. There was no safety net to catch them. Some did; some didn't.

After a period of time, Bob realized he could no longer stay and plead with the passengers who wouldn't. In order to survive, he had to jump because he knew the fuel was going to blow at any second. He did and it did. He jumped 40 feet to the ground and continued moving around working with survivors without even being aware that he had broken his ankle.

Later he was given the President's Award, one of only seven ever awarded by Pan American Airline. The citation: "In recognition of his courageous conduct and compassionate activity at the time of the tragic accident at Tenerife Island, March 27, 1977. Ignoring a broken ankle suffered in jumping from the shattered cockpit, he immediately organized able bodied survivors to help assist other passengers to safety and helped litter carriers evacuate the critically injured. His actions saved lives. His courage warrants public recognition."

How our brain perceives our world determines what we accomplish. Bob responded heroically during the crisis of two jumbo jets colliding because he had a high self-image and he interpreted the crisis as a call for action.

Bob accepted the problem as a challenge and was energized. People with a high self-image see a problem as a hurdle—something to be leaped over, not a barricade—an obstruction closing a passage. The level of challenges we accept determines the level of accomplishment we achieve. People with positive self-images say "I will try" and when problems come, as they do in anything we try, they simply try harder or try another way. People with a negative self-image don't put much effort into a project because they don't expect to be able to do it anyway. When problems come, they weaken their efforts to make it work instead of trying harder. The problems reinforce what they thought in the first place.

People with positive self-images have learned, or chosen, to react to their brains' exciter neurotransmitters. People with low self-esteem have learned, or chosen, to react to their brains' inhibitor neurotransmitters. People can be trained in a calm time before a tragic event to see such an event as a call for action. Norman Cousins, noted author and researcher, states that a panic reaction is natural in the wake of a disaster just as it is when a person is faced with catastrophic illness. He explains that although panic sends a hormonal surge to the heart, through training and preparedness individuals may learn to perceive a catastrophe as a challenge. He explains that challenge fixes the mind on new options and produces excitement connected to the achievement of new goals. People who regard difficult situations as an energizing challenge are in a good position not just to cope with catastrophe but to exert a measure of leadership in converting the panic of others into rational and lifesaving responses.

Training is available, but it is not the deciding factor. Decision is. Just as a person has a choice and must choose between AC or DC electrical power to make an appliance run efficiently, a person has a choice of which power source he or she plugs in to—energizing neuromessengers or anesthetizing neuromessengers. At times in our lives one is appropriate; at times the other is necessary. Sometimes, in reaction to trauma, our brain overproduces one or the other automatically.

Bob says his company provided no counseling for the crew or passengers after the crash. This was before the days of better diagnostic tools which are now allowing professionals to learn more about how the mind actually works and about the importance of releasing molecules produced at the time of a crisis. Then, accepted policy for a victim or first responder of a disaster was to deliberately try to put the tragedy behind and get on with one's life. The coping skill Bob chose, because it was the only one most people realized they had in those days, was avoidance. He was back to work in four months. When asked during an international television appearance thirteen years after the crash "How do you deal with the horrific memory imprinted in your brain?" he replied "I just suppress it. You just have to suppress it and get on with your life." In Bob's version of "getting on with your life" he volunteered to fly troops to the Gulf Crisis. He started by flying the first planeload from his area in Southern California and flew a total of over 4,000 troops.

Now, Bob has become a living example of hope for people who are hurting. He is spreading the word that there is hope for people whose lives have drastically changed after traumatic experiences, those who still, years after the disaster, have free-floating, unidentified, feelings. There are steps survivors themselves can take to start on the road back to full health and calm.

<u>Awareness</u> is the first step. The door opens when a person who is hurting finds out that there are people with similar problems who have found the way out of the pain.

<u>Decision</u> is the second step. One must make a personal decision to find out how other people identified and exorcised their pain.

<u>Action</u> is the third step. It is necessary to cross the threshold from awareness to actively going through steps to admit, identify and release the stress.

The grief process is one of the most effective tools for moving from avoidance to release of stress. The steps are painful. The reason the mind anesthetized the feelings in the first place was because they were too painful to handle. They are not any less painful during the grief process, but because time is not a factor, the memory can be released in manageable doses.

Bob's approach to Post Traumatic Stress is to release it gradually over a period of time. Just as there are two ways for depositing chemicals that stimulate an emotion in our bodies (through one dramatic identifiable event or through low-level stress built up over an extended period of time), there are also two ways tension-causing chemicals are released. Stored body memories may crash to the surface explosively. After having been stored for years, or even decades, an event in the present may trigger their release. That's the way it happens with some people. On the other hand, there are people who find relief from emotional pain the same way they find relief from a painful boil. An event in the present lances the protective covering which, in the case of emotional pain, is the wall of denial. A little pain oozes out. Some tension is released but then, as happens with a boil, the covering closes over again. The onset of Post Traumatic Stress Disorder does not always occur right after a catastrophe. People are different, and their reaction times are different.

Bob lives with an emotional aftermath of trauma. He also lives with the knowledge that, when presented with a problem, he thought of himself as part of the solution.

On the flight back from California, I was flying high. I thought my life had turned around. The book was being well received and, more importantly, I had opened up to the possibility of friendships again. After isolating for three years, for the last month I had let my barriers down and let people get close again. Victory over sadness was definitely in sight. I found I liked the feeling.

Chapter IX

ACCEPT DEFEAT BY OTHERS OR NEW CHALLENGES: THE CHOICE WAS MINE

Victory eluded me. Instead, storm clouds gathered. When I got back from California, momentum was high. The book was selling nationally, with even an international order coming in now and then. It was being surprisingly well received considering the fact that, except for the last two weeks, there had been no publicity other than word of mouth. I had made a mistake by not sending out pre-publication review copies because I had not known I should. Now, however, I had a team helping me learn about promotion and helping me carry through on plans. For the first time in my life I began to feel challenged by a problem rather than feel, as I had been trained in childhood to feel, that I was incapable of filling my own needs. Something new was building inside me. Yes, I had a lot of problems but, for a change, I also had hope. Chemicals produced in my brain gave me energy to try to hurdle them.

I learned that there are two types of promotion, (pre-publication promotion and continuing promotion after the promotion date) and that the most important promotion should have been done during the six months before publication. I had missed the first but now I started full speed on the second.

Then, I began to notice strange things happening. At first they seemed like little things, and seemingly unconnected. The owners of the printery began to have problems in their marriage and didn't get my press kits finished. Press kits are packets of information sent out to the media—to TV and radio interview program directors, to newspapers, and to magazines that print book reviews. Without press kits, publishing a book is much like wetting your pants in the dark. It gives you a nice warm feeling, but nobody knows about it.

The books sold so fast I needed a second printing after three months. I noticed that the process of getting the second run printed was not going as smoothly as the first. As it turned out, there were reasons I didn't yet know about. The press was facing bankruptcy. The financial stress resulted in the owners divorcing. Work was just not flowing through the press as in the past. Also, the book distributor was playing financial games with the publishers. The company was eventually taken over by another distributor and we all got paid a percentage of our invoices, but that was much, much later.

In trying to sell a piece of land in another state, I found out that I had been charged taxes on the manufacturing plant across the street instead of on my vacant land. It took time, money and energy to fight that.

And, to top it off, this was the time shakiness in my inheritance investments began to show up. I took my portfolio to a friend who was a stockbroker in a company other than the one that had sold them to me. He opened it, saw what investments I had and, without taking his eyes off what he was reading, reached in his drawer for his telephone book. As he started looking up a number I asked

EMILY: What are you looking for?

BROKER: I'm on the board of Woman Aware. I'm looking for their number to call and make an appointment for you. We'll talk about this portfolio later, but right now you need a job. There's nothing here. I've had clients come to me with these investments. I don't need to read it. I know what it says.

EMILY: What's Woman Aware?

BROKER It's an organization partially funded by United Way. It helps women like you who are not aware of their potential to become aware of it, then learn how to reach it. (He called and made an appointment for an hour from then.)

You've got nothing. You have no way to continue the lifestyle you were living when you were married, or even after you were divorced but had an inheritance. I advise you to get a job, sell your house, and move into subsidized housing.

Later, he arranged for a real estate broker to come out, look around the yard, go through the house room by room, measure it, and work up her estimate of the selling price. That day, however, I went directly to Woman Aware. The women there were, indeed, very aware. Women like me come in and out of their office every day. For starters, they were quite aware that I was not the only lady who had just come into an inheritance, had been advised by this same company, and who was now broke. I, like most women my age and older, had been raised in a culture where women were not taught money investment principles. For example, I literally had to teach my sixty year old mother how to write a check after my father died. Now, women like me are having to live with the consequences of that. Now we are expected to know, and looked down on for not knowing, things we were never taught.

I had enrolled in a class given by an established, well-known brokerage firm to learn money management. Instead, what I learned was that not all established firms were reputable in the 1980's decade of greed.

Debbie, my counselor at Woman Aware, taught me experientially by sharing some of her experiences with me. Some of her entry-level job stories were horror stories. As I saw similarities between us, I could feel my stomach lurch. I wasn't just being told about being broke, I was being helped to experience the feelings and learn how to handle them just as soldiers are trained before being sent into battle. Debbie took me through a Being Broke Boot Camp with all the expertise of a seasoned Drill Instructor. Fire drills are designed to give school children the same opportunity to avoid panic.

DEBBIE: After I went through a divorce, I had children to raise. Having an income was imperative, but I had little experience to write on an application. I tried and tried to get work, but I couldn't. I finally had to go the route of doing temporary work. I suggest you immediately register with a company that supplies temporary workers for other companies while you look for a permanent job. Working for a temporary agency is hard work because it's like having to go through the stress of adjusting to a new job every week or so. With each new assignment you'll have to adjust to a new office, new people, and new routines. Some of the jobs are entry level of the work force. You may be uncomfortable doing them, but they are all honest work, and they all provide an income.

Your talent is in your writing, public speaking, teaching in workshop format, and in secretarial skills. I suggest you send a resume to the three colleges in town, and to three or four in commuting distance. With three college degrees, you're going to have a hard time getting a job.

EMILY: I know what you mean. When I approach people to apply for an entry level job and they find out about my three college degrees, they tell me no because I'm overqualified. When I try for jobs at the level of my qualifications, they say no because I have no experience.

DEBBIE: Exactly.

EMILY: When I write on a topic that is new to me, I try to tie in with a college because a lot of people don't believe you know something unless you've learned it in a traditional classroom setting. Nowadays, people are realizing that more is retained when people actually experience something than when they're told about it and required to memorize facts. I've done a lot of writing, so I have a lot of degrees. They're like union cards, that's all.

DEBBIE: And, your age is against you. Although people don't come out and say that because there are laws against it, it is true.

There is a Christmas Craft Fair next month at the Convention Center. I want you to get a booth and sell your books at the Craft Fair.

EMILY: Me? Sell my books at a craft fair with the baked goods and appliquéed door stops?

DEBBIE: Yes. I also want you to contact printing companies in town to see if you can find one who will do your printing on vendor credit. You need to change printers and get your promotional material out to people.

When I left Debbie's office, I registered with a temporary worker agency. Then, I went to the Convention Center. I did not want to do that but felt I was safe because I figured they wouldn't have any spaces left anyway by this late date. At first the lady turned me down because my book was not a craft. I disagreed. I argued that I was a word crafter, the book was about the people of Siouxland, and I plied my craft in Siouxland. I thought I should qualify. I convinced her, but then she turned me down because there were no spaces left. Boy, was I relieved! As a formality, I asked if she would put my name on a waiting list in case someone canceled. She said she would, but that I would have to go over to City Hall and fill out the paper work. I said I would. She called over there and told them I was coming. In the time it took me to walk the few blocks from the Convention Center to the City Hall someone canceled! I was trapped. I felt panic but I knew my situation was so desperate I had to try all avenues. I filled out the application form and paid my reservation fee. After four hours I went back and told Debbie I had done the four things she told me to do.

DEBBIE: You did WHAT?

EMILY: What's the matter? I thought that's what you told me to do.

DEBBIE: I did, but I figured it would take you about four weeks, not four hours.

She hadn't told me that. My new life had started. I now stood at a fork in the path, and I didn't know which path I would be allowed to go down. One led to selling my home, moving into subsidized housing, giving up the project of my book and many of the other dreams I'd built up through the years. The other led to trying to save my home, and not giving up my lifestyle but trying to adjust it to one in which I could fill my own needs by my own productivity. The second path was a real risky one because, by any logical evaluation, I knew I would probably lose my home if I chose that one. But, hadn't I lost it already? At this point, hadn't I already lost my home and all my dreams? Yes, realistically, I had.

I had lost it all—my marriage, my lifestyle, my ability to keep my home, my independence. As each event had happened I had sunk deeper and deeper into depression. One night I was sitting in the dark in the living room watching for the real estate agent. It was a cold winter night. The streets and sidewalk had a sheet of ice on them. I saw her drive up in her Mercedes, wrapped in a beautiful full length fur coat. I watched her as she struggled up the steps and walk, slipping—recovering her balance—then sliding again. Armed with an electronic measuring gun, she was here to take my lifestyle away from me.

My reaction shocked me. A battle started inside of me as voices screamed, one after another:

I hope you fall.

How dare you come here representing a lifestyle I used to have to take it away from me?

I used to have a Mercedes and dress in stylish clothes. How dare you drive a Mercedes to take it all away from me?

The more the voices screamed accusations at her, the madder I got! I know now, though I didn't then, that was the key. Anger is the second stage of grief. Anger is the energy that cracks the wall of denial and avoidance of the shock stage of grief. Anger was the energy that made a hole in the wall so I could peek out and see the path to a new life—a life that was, hopefully, not dependent on subsidized housing. I think now, though I didn't realize it then, that something snapped inside of me and released a burst of new energy. I think now that burst of energy annihilated my feeling of hopelessness. I didn't realize that my journey through my emotions after a trauma had turned around that cold winter night. All I knew then was that after that, when anybody tried to discount me, or my feelings, or my abilities, I got mad. I got real mad.

Boy, I must have been non-verbally transmitting all this because when I got her written estimate it was a disaster. Luckily, I had gotten three agents to give me estimates, so I had something to compare it to. Although we walked through the house room by room and she whipped out her little gun and shot the opposite wall giving her accurate measurements in each room, her estimate completely left out one whole floor! That makes a difference in the selling price!

Friends pitched in and helped me design a booth for the Christmas Fair at the Convention Center. They even came and worked in it that week-end. The other crafters treated me as one of their own. When the fair ended, they talked me into entering one to be held the following week in another state. When I objected, saying there would be no vacancy this late, I was assured they'd fit me in. It ended up that people moved tables around in order to fit mine in.

The two craft fairs paid my November house payment. I sold a piano to pay for my December payment. My ever realistic friend Carolyn said "That's okay, Emily. Then when they repossess your house, that'll be one less thing you'll have to decide what to do with."

I began working for the temporary agency. The day of my first assignment I had to cancel out on a luncheon with the Symphony Guild, but I dropped off the food I had prepared for it on my way to work. I couldn't tell them where I was going because I had been told not to make that information known. Little did I know what the job was going to turn out to be. I was to report to the District Attorney's office. There was a large group in the room. I assumed that they were all from the temporary service, so I was surprised when the man in charge asked the lady next to me "You have your gun ready?" It seemed the permanent workers were going on a drug bust at a local bar and restaurant, arrest the owners and take government possession of it and its contents. The temporary workers were needed to take inventory, to count every bottle of beer, every knife, fork, spoon, and every Snickers bar. That night I cringed when the pictures of the event were shown on the evening news. There I was, (in the same easily identifiable clothes I had worn to deliver the food to my symphony friends), in a bar that was being busted rather than eating lunch with them. The news didn't clarify that I was there to count Snickers bars.

My next assignment was with Legal Services, an organization that helps low income people who cannot afford to pay a lawyer. I was uncomfortable because I was used to socializing with one of the lawyers, not typing up his dictation at almost minimum wage. I didn't have to worry. Joe introduced me around to everybody in the office and even talked others into buying some of my books. Friends are friends. As I typed up the case histories and record of help and advice clients were being given, I thought "These are exactly the same problems I'm having. Boy, this advice they're getting is good advice." I applied some of it to my own situation.

The day after I finished that assignment, I took my time sheet into the temporary agency office. They had another assignment they wanted me to go on immediately. A manufacturing company had fallen behind on work on their manuals and had called in for some people to "do a little work on their manuals." Since I was a writer, the agency thought I would be a useful person for the assignment. I went straight from their office to the plant. The lady from Human Resources offered to walk with me to the work site. As we walked, she said "Tomorrow, perhaps you will want to wear something more . . . er . . .comfortable." I'm a board member of the Sioux City Symphony Guild, had just come from a board meeting, and was still dressed in the clothes I had worn. I looked around at the workers. She meant: "Tomorrow, wear blue jeans."

The "little work on the manuals" turned out to be assembling manuals—the first chapter from this box, the second chapter from that box, the third chapter from the next box, etc. . This work was an experience in the publishing business I had not had before. Jan, the other lady the agency sent, pulled rank on me the whole time we worked there together because she arrived ten minutes before I did. She was working on her Masters in Learning Disabilities. I already had my Masters in Learning Disabilities. We were definitely overqualified, but we needed the money so we kept our mouths shut, hoped nobody would find out, and put those chapters in those binders. Well, I didn't exactly keep my mouth shut. I was fascinated by what they were making there and kept asking questions.

FOREMAN: If you keep asking questions, I'm going to promote you up to that next room.

EMILY: What's in there?

FOREMEN: The production line.

I looked around. If I had to be "promoted" to get "up" to the production line, where was I working now? That was the first time that my brain had allowed me to process some very obvious information. I was working, and one of my jobs was sweeping floors around my work station, in a warehouse.

The company was a young, growing one. Because of it's success, it was expanding rapidly and moving into a new building. The racks, shelves and parts weren't in the warehouse yet. My life had fallen from socializing at the very highest level, including the White House in Washington, DC, to sweeping floors in a warehouse in order to earn money for my basic needs. In addition, just as much of the modern equipment was not in place yet, many of the modern awareness resulting from men and women working together were not in place yet either. My friend and I were the only women working there at the time. Before the assignment in that warehouse was completed, I learned a lot about life in the real world.

One of the first things that I noticed was that this woman and I had a different range of vocabulary than the men. With them, everything was the fucking this and the fucking that, with no thought to careful selection or to nuances of their words. I doubt that any one of those men in that warehouse owned a thesaurus. They also used a lot of sign language, but it wasn't the sign language taught in our Learning Disabilities curriculum for use in trying to communicate ideas to the deaf. In the society I was raised in, anger was not acceptable in a lady so I just smiled and endured.

One day, I was sitting at my table doing "a little work on the manuals." I needed another box of one of the chapters, so got up and left the table to get it. No sooner had I gotten up than one of those clowns came zipping around the corner on a forklift, knocked my table over and sent everything asunder. If I had been sitting there, he would have knocked me asunder too. But, I didn't get angry. I just smiled and endured.

With this incident, something happened inside me. It was the birth of an awareness that my experience in the present definitely conflicted with my stored image of a lady's behavior. One day, as four of us were sitting at the table, the two men were discussing stealing condoms from a local department store and what they did with the condoms after they stole them. My friend got up and ran to the bathroom, but my "lady's" composure broke. I just sat there and spewed all over them. After that, there was still a wall between the two of us and the men in the warehouse, but for me it was no longer an interior wall. There was an imaginary sign on my imaginary wall that the men could all read: "Don't rattle my cage again."

Things ran smoothly for a while after that. One day when things started to heat up again I just blew. I didn't realize at the time how much courage it took for me to do that considering my background training had been that it was not all right to set boundaries on how people treat me. I just stood up and said "Look, guys, one thing I've learned here is that you can't let people run over you because if you do, out here they run over you with a forklift. So, I want you to know that's not going to happen to me again. From this day forward, I intend to stand up for myself and take care of the fucking situation!" The men were shocked at my language because they'd never heard me use it before, but they got my point. It didn't sink in to me until after I had finished that assignment that, after that day, the men had not only stopped using words around me that offended me but were actually saying please and thank you. I guess the incident that stands out most in my mind happened one day when I was tearing down the aisle not looking where I was going and ran straight, body on, into one of the men. I looked up and said "Oh, I'm sorry." In the past, this would have set up a whole pattern of innuendoes, but there was no tinge of disrespect in his voice as he expressed his feelings "No problem, mam, I kinda enjoyed it."

By the end of the assignment, I had learned two of life's most important lessons. I had a right to set limits on how people treat me, and I was capable of doing it.

The next crisis came when my house taxes came due. Up until that point, I thought that working in a warehouse assembling technical manuals for a manufacturing company was the pits. It wasn't. Working for a company that assembled their printed material for advertisements was worse. I went back to the temporary agency. I needed a job.

OWNER: I don't have any jobs I can send you on at the moment, but I'll call you when one comes in. I only have one thing right now, and it's not your type of job.

EMILY: If it's honest work and it pays money for taxes, it's my type of job.

OWNER: I won't send you on this one, Emily

EMILY: You have a job, I need the money. You are going to give it to me.

We stared each other down for a while and then, because he was smarter than I was, he said "Okay, I'll send you out on it, but it's not your type of job."

I knew what he meant the minute I walked in. For one thing, although I was dressed down appropriate for a warehouse job, I was as overdressed for this job as I had been with my Symphony Guild Board Member clothes on when I first walked in the warehouse for that other assignment. As far as I could see, there were workers in groups of five standing around tall tables gluing packets together. These were to be inserted and bound in as a page in magazines to advertise the products of the manufacturing plant I had worked in before. Many of the people didn't speak English, but English was not required because we were doing a task that could be shown without verbal explanation. My table put a bead of glue around three edges of a page, then folded it over. The first thing I learned was that glue from a hot glue gun is hot. I burned my hand early.

By noon, I knew that the owner of the temporary agency was right. I couldn't do this, and I went home for lunch along with a lot of other people who were not intending to come back either. I had given up. This was something I couldn't handle. When I got home, I had a letter in the mail box from the assistant managing editor of a major magazine who had read *Souls On Board*. The letter was in answer to a query letter I had sent him asking if I could write an article based on the book. He wrote back and said no, it was too similar to an article they had coming out, but that the topic of Post Traumatic Stress mentioned in the book interested him. I already knew this was a topic of great general interest because, by this time, I had begun getting calls and letters from readers that I had never met. Most were asking: "Now that you have made me aware of the symptoms of Post Traumatic Stress and the need for dealing with emotions after a trauma, what can I do about it?"

In his letter, he assured me that it was an extremely long shot, but that if I wanted to write an article, he would be willing to read it. The letter was typed and signed, but apparently overnight he had a change of heart. There was a handwritten PS added later that said "No, on second thought I think this is really too much of a long shot." Well, my answer to that letter was a "quit telling me no and give me a definite answer" letter. I told him I didn't care how long a shot it was, that if he would read it I thought the article was important enough to write no matter what the odds. His answering letter said, basically, go for it as long as you understand how iffy it is. I did and I did.

So, here I was home at lunch, ready to give up on my dream of trying to adjust my lifestyle rather than give up on it. What his letter brought to me in the mail was hope. I quickly evaluated the situation. I had indeed stood up four hours on a cement floor in a big building with many, many other people. I had indeed survived multiple hot glue burns on my hands because it took me a while to learn how to use the gun. I had indeed learned a few Spanish and Vietnamese words. The letter had indeed breathed into me a second wind. Now, I had to make a decision about what I was going to do.

Chapter X

MAPPING OUT A NEW OFFENSIVE

I went back and finished out the day. As I was leaving at the end of the day I decided I would come back the next day if given the option. I sweated out that evening. I truly expected a call telling me not to come back because I was too slow. Production line workers are much faster at putting hot glue around three edges of the page than I am. The call did not come. I was allowed to stay on the assignment. The whole time I was there I lived with the fear that I would be one of the people the supervisor quietly came up to and dismissed on the spot for being too slow. After a week or so I asked her about it.

SUPERVISOR: Yes you are slow. But, you are steady. You're always at your table and working on time, and you stay there working steadily. You take only the authorized breaks and don't spend time socializing from one table to another. I'm going to keep you as long as pace of the project allows me to.

The group at the table was evaluating me. One day they were talking (in front of me but not to me) about me and a man I'd been talking with the day before. They were discussing how he was trying to put the make on me. This caught me off guard.

EMILY: Put the make on me?

GROUP: Well of course.

EMILY: (Face shocked) I knew he was being friendly.

GROUP: (Laughing) Yes, Emily, he was being very friendly.

Then they discussed it (in front of me) and decided I needed help because I had absolutely no "street smarts". I realized later, from other incidences that I saw happen in the building, that a person with no street smarts could be a danger to the whole group. Unless I knew, and followed to a T, the accepted rules and patterns of behavior, I could start a race riot with knives, guns, and whatever. They told me, to the word, what the man would say when the subject came up. And, they told me exactly what to say, if I chose not to accept his invitation at that time, so as not to offend him or his race. He eventually said exactly what they said he would say; I said exactly what they told me to say; and we all went on putting hot glue around three sides of the pages.

After that, they taught me other things. They told me I was wearing the wrong kind of shoes for standing eight hours on a cement floor because they didn't have the proper cushioning. They told me what kind had cushioning to keep my legs from getting tired.

I learned a lot about people pulling together as a team instead of trying to do everything alone, as is often the case at the competitive executive level. At the time, I was living alone in an eight bedroom house. Some of them were living eight in one bedroom. I learned that it was not uncommon for many people to join together to live. Because not all were able to get steady jobs, it was the custom for people who were employed at the moment to support the group during the time it took others to find work.

I learned that the private, invisible walls people often put around themselves were not necessary in their group. In their group, people knew everything about each other. The key was that they accepted the reality of the way each person was. People in the group didn't have the ability to hide, but they didn't have the need to either because of this acceptance.

I learned a lot about the stress of living such an unpredictable lifestyle. I saw people with serious medical problems who kept working even though in pain because they needed the money. Even if they had sick leave which allowed them to take time off, they had no access to doctors. I learned what the sudden hush and recognizable look on a person's face meant when someone that the underground knew was connected with the immigration department walked down the aisle.

One day, when we were on break, I saw the tenderness on the owner's face when he knelt down by the woman next to me and put his arm around the back of her chair.

OWNER: I understand that when I work the group overtime, you get into trouble when you get home. Let me know if you see you are going to have a problem. I will see that you get off in time not to. (As he got up, he added) And tell that to anybody else you know who might be having a problem.

There was a look of bewilderment on my face. The woman was an adult. I knew she didn't live with her family. What kind of problem would she have if she didn't get home at a certain time? (Another woman leaned over to me.)

WOMAN: If you don't get back on time when they let you out of prison to work for the day, you lose the privilege.

I was warned one day to walk out of the building quickly after work, keep my eyes down and make no eye contact with anyone, go directly to my car, get in and leave. The underground had reported that the mother of a woman who had been fired was in the parking lot with a weapon waiting for the woman who had caused the problem and not gotten caught. I learned how much time and effort at minimum wage it can take to earn enough money to go to a Itzhak Perlman Benefit Concert. When I was living on money generated by an inheritance, I had not realized what the ticket price could represent. At a symphony reception my friend said

BOB: I watched you as you moved around the room. I could feel how much you enjoyed talking with people, and how much they seemed to enjoy being with you. I couldn't help but wonder what some of your friends here would think if they knew that you had been standing up eight hours on a cement floor before you came.

I knew what he meant. After I lost my inheritance, some of my friends were still there, some weren't. The assignment I was on now was giving me a clearer perspective of what's important and what Pam would call "the small stuff" in life. The most important thing I was learning was about community—about the interdependence of humanity.

As an author, I was only used to seeing—and thinking about—the finished book. I had never thought about how many varied people's efforts and attitudes contribute to my success. The people I met there were doing quality work in the publishing field, were proud of it, and having fun doing it. Now, when I see a new book in a bookstore, hot off the press, I often think about them. My concept of Portfolio People, (people I define as people in many different locations all with needed skills making up a team working on a single project), definitely expanded during this assignment.

After that experience, I became more open to the idea of sharing my home with people. During the time it had provided the background for the many activities of our family as three sons grew to manhood, it had been alive. During the time I had been grieving the loss of my marriage, it had been a sheltering cocoon, providing me with privacy for my tears. I had been alone but not lonely, just numb. Now, as feeling began to return, I found it lonely. I opened the door a crack. I agreed when two young professional women asked to move in with me. Dawn, the County Naturalist who had taught me to cross country ski, and her roommate Colleen, an Exercise Physiologist at the clinic a block away, expanded my world. They soon brought home Karen, a Physician's Assistant. Then, all three of my sons came home to visit—bringing their loved ones. Suddenly, after living alone in an eight bedroom house for four years, there were eleven people in the house, not counting carpenters, plumbers and electricians repairing things that the stress of so many people put on the ninety-eight year old Victorian lady of a house I lived in.

In order to work on the magazine article, I became more selective in the assignments I accepted. I only accepted assignments that would leave me energy at the end of the day to work on it. I worked for a lawyer for a while, in the office of a steel manufacturing plant, and on a religious fund raiser.

One day, as we were eating breakfast in the kitchen, one of the ladies who now lived with me said

COLLEEN: You should put my story in your book. Post Traumatic Stress is more than just stress after an airline crash or after Vietnam.

EMILY: I know that Colleen. I didn't know you had gone through a trauma. What kind of trauma?

Then this vivacious, beautiful long blond-hair young woman, who gives the impression on the outside that she's never had a care in the world, told me a story that absolutely stunned me.

COLLEEN: When I was a graduate student in Exercise Physiology at an urban university, I was running on a jogging trail near the school. I knew that the university was in a high-crime area and I had been warned to live by rules of caution while living there. However, coming from a small rural town in Iowa, I didn't think running in the broad daylight at 10:30 in the morning on a bright, sunny day posed a danger. I saw the man approaching me from the opposite direction, but thought nothing of it. As we met, he pulled a gun and, putting it to my head, threatened my life. He led me away from the trail, threw me on the ground and began beating me with the gun. I felt excruciating pain. I tried to break away, but he picked up a beer bottle and threatened me with it. I pretended to be passive. As he began to fondle me, he put the gun and bottle down. Although I realized they were within arms reach, I continued to play passive and bide my time until I saw my moment. Then, I broke away and grabbed the gun.

We struggled intensely for it, with the advantage passing from one to the other. I felt a burst of uncommon strength and was able to break away and run. He reached down, picked up the beer bottle from the ground and took out after me. When he caught up with me again, he broke it over my head, gashing it, and began slashing me. Blood filled my eyes, completely soaked my white tank top shirt, shorts, and almost every stitch of clothes I had on. I was still determined to survive. I kept running as fast as I could. Glancing over my shoulder to see how close he was, I saw he had not pursued. I saw him leisurely strolling away in the other direction.

Chapter XI

THE UNDERLYING TRAUMA OF HIGH-CRIME AREAS

In our country today, some neighborhoods are exploding into vicious battlefields. The Los Angeles riots of 1992 were not about racism. Rodney King just happened to be black. The real issue was an explosion of feelings against a system that lets some people in and keeps some people out. Such a system does not fit into the balanced wheel our lives need in order to keep them running smoothly. The three points of mind, body and soul are not given equal focus. Such a system gives little, if any, focus to the area of soul, an area which involves sharing without coercion. In fact, in such a system, sharing without coercion can often be counterproductive.

The Los Angeles riots started in the area of feelings as a cry against police brutality by people assigned to live the "somebody has to be lower" role. They quickly exposed a deeper layer of feelings. Looting took over as a cry went up for more justice in the area of the body, the area of material things, and for relief from the effects of the ruling class' instruments of control: police and courts, the economic system, educational institutions, and health care systems.

People who have not felt the intense feelings and have no experience with the ticking time bombs that many high crime neighborhoods are mined with can get hurt. Colleen did. People who live with continual doses of fear and anxiety, whether it be stimulated by a source they are conscious of or a source buried in their subconscious mind, live in constant trauma.

COLLEEN: I went to the hospital but didn't stay overnight. A girlfriend came and got me. I went home with her and she took care of me. I called my parents the next day, told them I'd been attacked, but didn't tell them how serious the attack had been. I let them know I was all right and well taken care of, and asked them not to come. The trip was long and there was nothing they could do since the crisis was over.

My boyfriend, also from Iowa, was in college about three hours away. Together, we had picked one far from home to finish our undergraduate work. After I graduated, I went on to graduate school at a university in the same state. I was attacked at the beginning of spring break at his college so he was off for a week. He came and spent the weekend with me, then went back to his campus.

Colleen dealt with her inner battle of emotions after a trauma in silence. She was able to quickly submerge her feelings and get on with her life. Although, at that time, the pattern had not yet become recognized, her relationship followed what is now considered a very predicable pattern for relationships after a trauma. It broke within a year or so.

People who live in high crime areas must equip themselves with equipment for survival. It is not GI Equipment (which means Government Issue Equipment), it is equipment they must custom design and develop themselves. The ability to detach from feelings when necessary is one of the tools needed.

Danger stimulates fear. Our body will not accept living in a constant state of fear and the continuous surges of adrenaline it triggers. It adapts by strengthening its ability to produce internal opiates to blunt feelings. Unfortunately, it isn't selective blunting. Feelings of fear are not the only feelings affected by the resulting detachment from feelings. Dr. Matthew Friedman, of the National Center for Post Traumatic Stress Disorder, says that physical changes seen in the brains of

Vietnam Vets may account for the emotional numbing (an inability to experience tender feelings) that often accompanies Post Traumatic Stress Disorder. This may also affect people who live in, or were raised in, high crime areas. It may affect their ability to form, or maintain, close relationships.

Although this highly efficient coping skill is not GI equipment, like GI equipment, it isn't needed after the intensity of war is over. When the truce is called, it can be adjusted to one with a lesser capability. When it is adjusted, personal relationships can be deeply felt again.

People who live in an area that has experienced an arson fire, or one susceptible to an arson fire, live in a high crime area. Nicely manicured lawns and intelligent neighbors notwithstanding, after such an event there is an associated constant undercurrent of fear of crime.

Lois was a member of the Santa Barbara, California, Emergency Services staff at the time of the Paint Fire tragedy, July 27, 1990. It was started by an arsonist below the crest of a mountain above town in an area called Painted Cave. It raged through Santa Barbara, destroying or damaging 648 structures (most of them single family homes) before being contained twenty three hours later. Another four days passed before it was controlled. Left with feelings of anger and frustration, Lois now lobbies hard to get arson fires that are declared a national emergency prosecuted as, and carry the penalties of, a federal crime.

She poignantly described the experience—and her feelings. She remembers the feeling of seeing the rubble where a community used to be. She recalls the eerie quiet as she later drove back through the burned area, returning to what had been her office only just an hour before. She remembers seeing small flames on both sides of the road continue to eat away at walls still standing after the fire roared through the canyons. Imprinted on her brain is the picture of a tree near the road as it exploded into flames.

Within fifteen minutes after the fire started, her boss had set up work stations in the Emergency Operations Center (EOC). After she and two other members of the Santa Barbara Amateur Radio Club arrived, he left them to continue the setup work while he went to the fire headquarters. When smoke began to get thick in the room, Lois dialed number after number. She wanted to ask someone to go to the roof and shut off the air conditioning fan to stop it from pulling smoke into the building. Unable to reach anyone, she decided to go look for someone. When she opened the security doors, however, she found out that smoke being pulled into the building from a distant fire wasn't the problem. The building she was in was in immediate danger. People were running. The call rang out "Evacuate! Go!"

After hurrying back to warn the radiomen, she did just that. Coming out of the building she saw that although it was only a little after six in the evening the parking lot was dark and, she recalls, beautiful in a strange way. She describes how feathery sheets of orange sparks from blowing, blazing palm fronds blew around her ankles and burned holes in her nylons. She saw her new car outlined against a 20 foot high wall of flame, and saw flames flickering in front of the hood. It took courage to get in the car and start the engine, but it was something she had to do. She had to get out of there quickly; there was fire everywhere.

Traffic was grid locked on the highway. Black clouds of smoke were racing nearer and nearer. Each road from the north was emptying more people and cars onto the already-blocked highway. The fire jumped Highway 101 and continued to burn. Fed by 40 to 60 mph wind gusts, it poured down from a mountain top in Los Padres National Forest to within a mile of the ocean in only 80 minutes, claiming as its victims one person dead, eighteen people hospitalized, and 4,900 acres burned.

The home of Barbara, Lois' close friend, was not threatened that time—but her emotion equilibrium was. It still is. Barbara Gaughan is a highly intelligent professional woman who heads her own public relations agency in Santa Barbara, Ventura and Hollywood and moderates a popular series called "PR Power Breakfasts." She is strong in the area of the mind. Now, however, in the area of emotions, just as everyone else in a high-crime area, she lives with one of the major symptoms of emotions after a trauma: an underlying, nagging uneasiness of "This happened before—it could happen again."

Barbara has powerful self-image resources to draw on.

BARBARA: I was the oldest of three daughters and went to an all girls' high school. I never heard of anybody else being a leader except women. That got imprinted on my brain. Also transmitted to me, and I guess imprinted on my brain, was the realization that my father really wanted a boy. I learned early to play the role of my father's son. I also learned early that when something needs to be done, just do it. I know I'm not perfect, but I'm close enough to get it done somehow. Anyway, perfection leads to procrastination. I'd never start anything if I thought I had to do it perfect.

Most people realize that a person's personality and past experiences influence his or her reaction to, and recovery from, the stress of problems like the death of a spouse or a divorce. In the past it was thought that extreme trauma was capable of producing mental disorder in anyone regardless of differences in personality or past experiences. Because early studies of PTSD were mainly of military casualties, torture victims, and prisoners of war, this seemed to be the case. Recently, however, a different picture is beginning to emerge as studies are being done on depression in the general public, on alcohol use and drinking problems, and post-traumatic stress resulting from lower level, continued doses of emotional or physical abuse in everyday life. If not identified and released, it accumulates over time.

At present, the official psychiatric classification of Post-Traumatic Stress Disorder (PTSD) links it only to "a distressing event that is outside the range of usual human experience." Dr. Naomi Breslau and fellow workers of the Henry Ford Hospital in Detroit and the University of Michigan Medical School thought the illness probably affected many more people than this narrow group. They wondered just how many people were affected by PTSD in addition to people covered by this definition. Surely there were other causes than such catastrophic events as a terrifying plane crash, an arson fire in their neighborhood, or Vietnam. Picking a random sample of young adults in the Detroit area to work with, the group asked about traumatic events the people had experienced and about whether or not they had developed the full symptoms of PTSD afterwards.

The events most commonly mentioned were being raped or physically assaulted, a serious accident or injury, or seeing someone else being killed or injured. After the experience, one in four people developed PTSD. They found that when a person was unable to do anything to stop the trauma, he or she was more likely to develop PTSD. Those identified by the workers on the Detroit study as being at greatest risk for exposure to traumatic events were:

1. Male sex
2. Less than college education
3. History of three or more early conduct problems
4. Neuroticism
5. Extroversion
6. Persons with a family history of any type of psychiatric disorders or substance problems

Early conduct problems were defined as:

1. got into trouble with teacher or principal frequently because of misbehavior
2. played hooky
3. repeated a grade

4. was suspended or expelled from school
5. ran away from home
6. told a lot of lies
7. started fights
8. had early sexual experience
9. used drugs

The problem of "early separation from parents" was defined as whether the person was brought up by someone other than parents for a period of four months or more before age sixteen. People with this problem were not found to be at higher risk for exposure to traumatic events but, if they got exposed, they were at a higher risk of developing PTSD.

The work of other scientists, too, shows the presence of PTSD caused by events associated with everyday life. One of the first, if not the first, report published on PTSD in the general population was of work done in St. Louis, Missouri, by Dr. John E. Helzer and fellow workers of Washington University. They put their focus on traumatic events that later caused typical PTSD symptoms. Although a lot of people have some symptoms of PTSD (such as hyper alertness and sleep disturbances) there is more to the illness than that. In addition to suffering from the recognized symptoms of PTSD, they also found that the risk for developing certain other psychiatric disorders was twice as great in people suffering from post-traumatic stress disorder as it was in people who weren't.

How can you tell if you are affected? Usually, people can tell if they are unhealthy because they feel pain. This is not always true in post-traumatic stress because of the factor of denial which is so much a part of the disorder. It is wise, in fact in most cases essential, to work through the problem together with a professional because a professional can often identify pain even when our mind has used denial as a tool to anesthetize us from feeling it.

A picture that is now developing is that there are factors that affect PTSD indirectly by increasing the chances of being exposed to traumatic events. Those who live in high-crime areas are at high risk for exposure to traumatic events. People who choose to earn their living as emergency medical technicians, military men or women, firemen, policemen, etc. put themselves at high risk for exposure to traumatic events.

Not all people who are exposed to traumatic events develop PTSD. Scientists working on the Detroit study found that, with the exception of rape, more than 75% of those exposed to typical traumatic events did not develop PTSD. According to findings presented at the American Psychological Association meeting in New York City, June, 1990, one in ten Americans has suffered the symptoms of the disorder.

Although not everybody exposed to a traumatic event develops post traumatic stress symptoms, 10% of our exposed friends and neighbors is still a lot of people—and a lot of pain.

Chapter XII

THE BATTLE CRY: CAN WE TALK?

(Names in this chapter have been changed to protect privacy)

The battle cry of the War Against Silence is "Can we talk?" The next person I talked to was Cricket. I talked to her about the silence victims of incest live with. In this life we don't get what we deserve, we get what we negotiate. Unfortunately, we can't negotiate to get our pain healed or our needs met until we can talk about them. We can't negotiate in silence. Talking helps us identify, admit and face that what is causing our pain really happened. . .and really happened the way it happened. Before we can tell someone else about a memory we must recall it. We must allow it to bubble up into our conscious thoughts and organize our thoughts about it. Our own defense mechanisms can alter our perception but have no influence on other people's perception of the reality of our situation. Speaking out runs our perception of a memory through a reality check.

Safe people are unbiased people. They reflect reality, not judgment. By talking, we establish connection with another human being. We're no longer alone with our memory—or our burden. It's necessary for people who are hurting to speak out, but it is not necessary to speak out in public. Tradition and society may try to put us in a prison of silence. Taboos on talking about the events are often imposed. Victims must remain silent; must remain in pain.

Our bodies, too, are equipped with a way to silence us. Things that are too painful to remember, we simply choose to forget. Often this is not a voluntary choice, or a choice we are even conscious of. It is something our body automatically does. Our bodies produce natural morphine-like opiates that anesthetize us until we are stronger. At this writing, my friend Cricket's brain has anesthetized her. She is now beginning to become aware of traumatic incidence of incest, but she can not yet remember who was involved.

As she reached adolescence, Cricket behaved like a bitch. She wasn't a bitch (which means a female dog); she behaved like a bitch. There's a difference between how a person behaves and what a person is. Cricket is a beautiful person, caring and warm, but she was incested as a child. Children who have been incested suffer from post traumatic stress. They continue behavioral patterns that allowed them to survive during their young years but prevent them from building healthy relationships when they get older.

That's the bad news. The good news is that new methods for recovering from post traumatic stress resulting from a traumatic childhood are now becoming apparent. During times of trauma, a function of the brain is to control production of chemicals of emotion. It is a biological response to a stimulus. Later, sometimes years or decades later, they can surface as body memories. Body memories are memories that have been stored in the body as chemicals on a level below our conscious memory. Cricket suffers from body memories stored in her body from a traumatic childhood in a dysfunctional family. Now she is having to face the reality that a childhood that seemed normal at the time, based on beliefs she was taught by her family and social institutions, was actually destructive to her ability to live a happy life. It has kept her from being able to form healthy relationships. Life rules physically imprinted on her brain by cellular changes, in response to teachings and experiences no longer remembered in her short term conscious memory, now influence her present day decisions. She has dissociated from the memory on the conscious level, but the chemicals are still active. They continue to stimulate nerve pathways on the subconscious level.

Cricket is now becoming aware that she was a victim of incest because, through therapy, memories of incidents are beginning to surface. It is now safe to go back and look at them through adult eyes, rather than the eyes of the child she was then, to resolve her body's conflict in response to these issues. She experiences momentary flashbacks that reveal incidents of sexual incest, but they are buried deeply and her mind fights hard to protect her from them.

Crossing of personal boundaries in children (with it's resulting confusion of personal identity) has as intense, if not more intense, an effect as the same act of emotional or physical rape in an adult. Two elements enter in with a child that are not factors with an adult:

> a child's added helplessness because of total dependence on adults to have needs met, and a child's immaturity due to lack of knowledge or experience in how to deal with this violation.

Cricket tends to reenact the abuse of her childhood by forming present day relationships which continue the abuse. Love is about chemistry. Sex is about physics. Children who have sexual feelings aroused in them by being fondled and touched in ways that are not appropriate when they are too young to understand the difference often never learn the difference. Incest victimization sets a person up to accept victimization as a battered spouse, promiscuous adult, or even a prostitute. Cricket was a battered spouse but remained with her husband through years of abuse. Growing emotionally strong enough to leave him, she continues to get into relationships in which she is abused. Although a highly successful professional woman, she has unidentified feelings of guilt and feels damaged and defective. Parts of her body sometime feel numb, not a part of her. She has out-of-body feelings, sensations of floating away from her body.

Building on a foundation of growing self-esteem resulting from graduating from school with honors, progressing up the ladder to an executive position in her field, and beginning to move in circles the salary from such a job allowed, she made the decision to get professional help. Only after participating in several abusive programs did she find a supportive program. With many people, therapy methods based on shame and humiliation aren't effective because they are abusive. If childhood abuse caused a problem in the first place, continuing abuse during therapy often has the effect of causing the brain to continue to produce protective anesthesia.

Until the growing understanding of the biological basis of behavior, the victim was usually placed in the role of inticer. Sigmund Freud and Alfred Kinsey of the Kinsey Report both placed the blame for incest squarely on the victim. Freud taught the theory of the Oedipus complex, the idea that every child between three and six years of age goes through a stage during which he or she sexually desires the parent of the opposite sex. Now, studying his previous work "The Aetiology of Hysteria," which he presented before his colleagues at the Society for Psychiatry and Neurology in Vienna, Austria, on April 21, 1896, some scientists are considering the possibility that the Oedipus Theory was an attempt to save his professional career. Freud hurt the credibility of his paper by stating that all mental illness results from childhood sexual abuse. Although the word "all" makes this statement untrue, there is evidence of enough cases where mental illness does result from childhood sexual abuse for that part to be considered valid. Because the paper presented in Vienna stated his belief that mental illness is the result of childhood sexual abuse (and used the words rape, assault, trauma, and attack to describe the abuse) his colleagues attacked, denounced and ostracized him. As a result, he retracted the Seduction Theory and developed the Oedipus Theory. The article "Incest, A Chilling Report" in February 1992 Lear's magazine gave me a new awareness of incest. I recommend it; it's informative and well worth reading.

In talking about the repetition of sexual contact between adults and preadolescents, the Kinsey team's famous 1953 report *Sexual Behavior In The Human Female* claims that the children became interested and more or less actively sought the repeated abuse. There seems little evidence to support that idea. How can a child initiate acts they are too naive to understand, and why would the child seek the repeated abuse when it often causes so much pain? The idea does not take into consideration the issues of power imbalancc, physical superiority, or economic dependence. When one looks at the reality objectively, what is seen is a picture of a tiny child or early adolescent in a situation of being asked, or forced, to fill the sexual needs of a large adult he or she trusts and is often dependent on for food and shelter. The realistic picture often includes a total betrayal of trust, a torn vagina or anus, or semen blocking flow of air through the throat just as completely as water blocks a drowning person's throat.

The reality is that adults, in any society, are charged with the responsibility of filling dependent children's needs and with teaching them skills, emotional responses and behavior patterns that will eventually allow the children to function in the society as responsible adults. Incest does just the opposite. Incest trains a child to accept victimization in adult life. Incest is a blatant statement to a child that he or she is not respected - is not worth much in the perpetrator's opinion. It is a statement made by a person responsible for helping to mold and develop personality and character at a time when the child's self-image is being formed. This opinion is absorbed by the child and becomes his or her self-image. Incest has a long lasting effect on the self-image, self-esteem, character, personality, and behavior pattern of its victims. In adult life, Cricket is left with the problems of sexual dysfunction, depression, and low self-esteem. Incest victims no longer view themselves in a positive light. They often blame themselves and, even though they are often highly successful people, live with a sense of worthlessness. Because of this self-blame and sense of worthlessness, incest victims are extremely vulnerable to re-victimization.

Cricket, having been trained in early life that her worth was in the role of filling the sexual needs of others, continued to behave that way when she reached adolescence. She attempted to buy personal relationships with sex. Now she can examine past events as an adult rather than as a small child who is powerless and totally dependent on adults to fill her basic need for food and shelter, let alone her emotional needs.

Cricket's brain has anesthetized the connections between her present behavior and experiences that taught her that this is her role. Now, as a result of therapy programs based on the new discoveries about the brain, body memories stored for years in her subconscious are rising to the surface and she is aware of them. Now, Cricket has a choice of how to react.

Her feelings . . . like little soft, delicate animals . . . have been trapped in her body for a long time. Now they have a chance to come out but, as is nature's way, they won't come out until they feel it is safe.

At the moment, Cricket lives the life of a dependent personality. Some people work through the inner conflict of trauma with dependencies and addictions. When a person, place or substance offers relief from the pain, even temporarily, most of us tend to behave the same way again. Some people eventually grow to depend on the behavior to mask the pain. They become addicted to a person's approval, to a place or to a thing, and become comfortable in the pattern temporarily. Problem is, addictions only mask, not resolve, a problem.

It is common for victims of child abuse to become promiscuous as adolescents or adults. Because a small child has no framework for understanding the sexual feelings generated in his or her body. Sex Education 101 becomes a teach-it-to-yourself course. She touches herself. When she touches a spot that feels good, she does it again . . . and again . . . and again. This is called masturbation. Then, she moves on to touching someone else. Touching someone else, and asking to be touched, is a common aftermath of incest. Victims display a knowledge and interest in sex that is inappropriate for their age. Often victims ask peers to engage in oral sex during play. This drives recess teachers up the wall, or up the fence if it happens to be a warm, sunny, take the kids out on the playground sort of day. With these behavior patterns, their right to refuse sex is often lost and they are repeatedly re-victimized.

Adults who have sex forced on them already have an understanding of what sex is. They have a basis for evaluating the particular incident. Sexual abuse of children, on the other hand, usually shapes their understanding of sex and feeling towards it and often shatters trust in the opposite sex.

This can lead to restricting social contacts to people of their own sex because that is the only sex they trust. As they get older, people who are comfortable only with their own sex are faced with an inner conflict of a sexual identity confusion, and with questions of "Am I homosexual?" When this happens to incest victims, there are often no healthy role models to follow.

When faced with feelings he or she is too immature to handle, a child struggles. As a survival mechanism, multiple personalities often begin to form. This intensifies the struggle as each one fights for control. To a much lesser degree, we've all experienced this same inner struggle.

> Inner Voice: I'll eat that piece of chocolate cake
> Other Inner Voice: No, if I do I'll gain weight
> Inner Voice: I could eat it and exercise long enough to burn off the number of calories
> Other Inner Voice: I don't have time in my schedule today to do extra exercise. . . and on . . . and on . . .

Just as friends who argue too long and intensely can split and end up with a wall between them and not talking to each other, our inner personalities can split up too. We can develop multiple personalities.

Traditionally, adults' responses to symptoms of incest have been to stigmatize the child and treat reactions that are natural consequences of incest as behavioral problems. Now, with new information, the response often is to recognize it as a warning flag of a relationship problem—often, but not always.

Some incest victims pull completely inside themselves and become totally anesthetized. Others ask for help by expressing their pain publicly. Most victims try a combination of both. Reactions of people around them quickly teach what pattern of behavior is necessary to survive in their culture. Cultures differ. Resulting patterns of behavior include: Chaotic inside (passive and withdrawn) and Chaotic outside: (workaholism, promiscuousness, criminal behavior).

Doctors David Finkelhor and Angela Brown of the Family Violence Research Program, University of New Hampshire, Durham, looked at the problem of sexual child abuse from the point of view of the child not as the inticer, but as a person going through traumatic stress. They identified four forces set in motion by sexual child abuse that produce traumatic stress. When people concentrate on these results of sexual child abuse, rather than focusing on trying to place the blame for what caused the incident, the victim has a better chance of getting the help he or she needs to recover from the effects of incest. The consequences of these forces, both emotional problems and behavioral problems, are easier to see and are easier to accept as natural outcomes of the abuse.

Each incident differs, and each child reacts differently depending on the memories and experiences already stored in his or her brain. One can't say a particular type of sexual abuse causes a particular type of reaction. However, an understanding of the effects, and possible outcomes, of these forces can lead to a clearer picture. Finkelhor and Browne identified traumatic sexualization, betrayal, powerlessness, and stigmatization.

TRAUMATIC SEXUALIZATION: Sexuality includes both sexual feelings and attitudes about sex. Traumatic sexualization refers to a process which has traumatic and harmful effects on a child's development of sexual feelings and attitudes. This can happen in a number of ways in incest.

When a child is given affection, attention, privileges and gifts in exchange for sexual behavior, he or she learns to use sex to manipulate people.

When an adult gets intense pleasure from fixing attention on a part of a child's body, the part is then given distorted importance and meaning in the child's mind.

In incest, the offender is one of the group with responsibility for teaching the child sexual morality. Incest generates confusion and teaches misconceptions. Traumatic sexualization also occurs later as anger and frightening memories of the events become associated in the child's mind with acts of sex.

Children are different, and the effects of traumatic sexualization vary not only from child to child but with the type of incest. Incest is not always as dramatic as to cause a torn vagina or teeth cuts on a penis. More subtle behavior, behaviors that traditionally have been accepted as expressing love in many families but are used in some instances to generate sexual feelings in the adult, also generate sexual feelings in the child. Certain behaviors generate sexual feelings in the child even when there is no deliberate attempt, or even awareness, on the part of the adult to do so. Sometimes, because these acts have always been done and accepted in a culture, an adult is not even aware of incesting a child. Incest, not always violent; sometimes is quiet and subtle. **Incest is anything that causes arousal and transmits the adult's sexual feelings to the child.**

Sometimes incest (defined as inappropriate sexual behavior between members of a family that generates inappropriate sexual feelings in either adult or child) are acts family members believe are expressions of love. Sadly, it is possible for an offender to generate sexual feelings in the child without being aware of the aftermath.

Finkelhor and Browne feel that a child can be harmed more in experiences in which the offender attempts arouse the child than if he or she simply uses the child to masturbate. Experiences in which the offender encourages the child to participate can be more harmful since it can later result in a feeling of guilt. A child who is not yet aware of the implications of the sex acts may be harmed less than a child who understands. When force is used, fear becomes associated with future sex acts.

BETRAYAL: Eventually, victims realize that someone they depended on has caused them harm. Even in cases where it was done unintentionally, the harm was done. Victims sometimes find themselves in the position of loving the person but hating the person's behavior. This is a difficult position to be in. The reality is hard to face, even harder to accept. However, inner peace will not come until reality is admitted and accepted. Acceptance does not mean forgetting. The event happened. The memory will always be there, consciously or subconsciously. The memory cannot be erased, but the chemicals stimulating painful emotions in response to the memory can be released. The process to release these painful emotions is the grief process. The loss of the illusion of that family member must be grieved just as surely as the loss of a family member through death.

The degree of betrayal is influenced by the degree of trust the child felt for the offender before the abuse. Abuse that confirms suspicions is not as damaging as an experience initially seen by the child as nurturing and loving. Children who are believed and supported when they break the silence are not as damaged as those disbelieved and ostracized.

A child can experience betrayal of different forms in incest. A child may come to realize that the offender was not telling the truth, was giving conflicting information, or simply misrepresenting standards of morality to manipulate the situation. In trying to get help, the child may be betrayed by other family members or friends. Often others are unable, or unwilling, to face the reality. When abused children try to get help, it has traditionally been common for them to be accused of making the story up or of feeling people's attitudes toward them change after they tell of the experience.

POWERLESSNESS: Powerlessness refers to a process in which a victim's will, desires and efficacy (power to produce an effect) are continually obstructed. Many things in incest contribute to a feeling of powerlessness. Incest crosses a child's personal boundaries because personal body parts are touched. Often the body is physically invaded.

Coercion, fear and manipulation are factors in incest. Often a child experiences disbelief and rejection after the experience, leading to a feeling of being trapped and unable to correct or escape the situation. Victims who are successful in getting help to control the situation seem to come out of the experience with less damage than those who are not.

STIGMATIZATION: Stigmatization refers to branding the victim with negative attributes: shame, guilt, differentness, badness, loose morals, damaged goods, etc. This negativism can be communicated in many ways. Some offenders blame and shame the victim. Others clearly point out is not the victim's fault but insist it be kept a secret. Pressure to "keep the secret" stigmatizes because it clearly establishes differentness.

Incest is a tragedy. Men and women who were incested as children live with an aftermath of unidentified pain until the molecules of emotion are released. Incest isn't always physical. Emotional incest can be just as stressful (sometimes even more stressful) than physical incest because it is less obvious. Physical incest is direct, emotional incest manipulation. Both, however, fill the needs of the adult, not the needs of the child.

A type of incest that is often unrecognized or not understood as being harmful is eroticism. Eroticism is inappropriately touching or fondling a young child in a way that generates sexual feelings in the adult. It also generates sexual feelings in the child. Some adults who do not have a satisfying outlet for their sexual drives within their peer group practice eroticism with their own children or children who have been placed in their care for training. Young single mothers, grandparents, and priests who have taken vows of celibacy among their peers are at high risk. So are parents who play the role of happily married on the outside but who are not having their needs met on the inside. An eroticised child is at high risk for developing erotomania, defined as morbid propensity to love or make love; uncontrollable sexual desire; melancholia caused by love. Melancholy is defined as morbidly gloomy; sad; dejected or suggesting or promoting sadness.

Eroticised children are knowingly or unknowingly used, in effect, as an object to masturbate with. The sexual feelings generated in them are far beyond what their physical or mental development is capable of dealing with. Dejection is a logical outcome of trying to handle such an impossible task. Dejection is defined as low or depressed spirits, disheartenment. Children who have been eroticised grow up to be dependent personalities—dependent on relationships. Their need to be in a relationship is so strong that they are incapable of standing up for their rights, or even recognizing that they have rights in relationships.

We cannot change past behavior—ours or anybody else's. That is an event. We can, however, choose to release stored emotions in order to change their consequences.

Moral values expressed by people of the culture, even if not practiced, often reinforce feelings of guilt and shame, particularly if family, friends or neighbors react negatively to the situation. Focusing on factors that caused the violation, rather than on trying to hide or fix blame, is far more helpful to the child, and to our society in general. At first glance, incest appears to be a moral issue. A closer look reveals elements of its being a learned habit spawned by hierarchy cultures that put a taboo on talking about the topic. This blanket of silence effectively shields the abuser from exposure and, more importantly, blocks any public consequences for the behavior. The victim is often re-victimized with the burden of guilt.

In most cases, people who abuse children were abused themselves as children. Habits learned through experience in childhood are learned vividly and are repeated, whether learned at a parent's knee or at parent's penis. Split personalities resulting from dissociation from the horror of childhood trauma are often as hidden from the abuser as from the abused. A second generation victim, now the abuser, also experienced and can repeat physical anesthetizing of unbearable trauma.

Before healing can take place, the victim must accept the fact that he or she has the Right to Relief. This is a right of both first generation abused or second generation abused who is now both the abused and the abuser.

Behaviors in the past cannot be changed. Things that happened in the past happened. . .period. Events of the past cannot be changed, but habits imprinted on the brain as a result of the experiences can. Memories and habits are imprinted on the brain by experiencing both thoughts and events. They are released and changed the same way: by re-experiencing thoughts and events.

In the past, the taboo placed by society on speaking out about horrific topics kept the victims of such tragedies Hostages of Horror. This does society no good because it just perpetuates the horror into the next generation.

Our bodies fight for balance in our lives. It is necessary to re-experience horrific experiences in order to release stored chemicals of emotion. If society throws a blanket of silence over re-experiencing the event verbally, the body may be forced to release the emotions through repeating the habits and behaviors. Incest victims, and perpetrators, have a Right to Relief. New information now being discovered because of recent advances in computer-assisted diagnostic equipment shows that it is not only possible, but shows how to do it. Mankind all over the world is in a period of breaking the taboos of silence on events that cause pain. Our world is in a period of transition now. Steps are beginning to be taken which can keep the pain from being passed down to the next generation. We are in a period in which it is possible to begin breaking the abused/abuser cycle by speaking out about pain.

The cycle of abused becoming abuser by re-enacting and becoming abuser is vicious. The pain is horrific in both stages. The healing, for both abused and abuser, can only begin when the silence is broken. The battlefield is identified. Let the **WAR AGAINST** such **SILENCE** begin!

Chapter XIII

TRAUMA, DISSOCIATION AND MULTIPLE PERSONALITY

People have asked me: "Since your book is about harmony, balance in one's life, and peace, why do you put it in the setting of conflict, and war?"

My answer is: There is a silent conflict of emotions going on in both abused and abuser. This conflict is on the subconscious level. I write about a War Against Silence because of this conflict. It is a battle to unmask and relieve the pain from secrets our minds keep. Wars are inevitable but the cause to rally around can be chosen. Winning this war is imperative because the ways some people are choosing to try to mask the pain of emotions after a trauma, such as:

alcoholism,
street or prescription drug addition,
promiscuity,
eroticism,
dependency on other people,
over or under eating,
over or under sleeping,
excessive gambling,
workaholism,
rigidity,
controlling, etc.,

are eroding the very foundations of our country, and countries all over the world.

This is a period in history when people are beginning to be able to speak out about the effects of emotions after a trauma. Until this period in history, the connection between emotions stored after a trauma and events happening in people's lives in the present was not understood. The importance of the area of feelings and self-esteem was not understood. Because of this, the necessity of, nor process for, breaking the cycle of behaviors generated by these emotions was not understood. Unless these emotions and the patterns they imprint on the brain are identified and released, the resulting behavior patterns they cause will continue to show up from generation to generation.

Habits will not be changed, nor will traditions and laws be changed, until people become aware that they need to be. The new facts reveal the necessity for adjusting our institutions, laws, etc. from control to communication. Control doesn't work because it is not based on how the brain actually works.

Our incest laws vary from state to state. Would our laws be the same as they are now if a two year old was able to express, and was listened to if she did, feelings such as:

"I feel terribly frightened when a man who towers above me forces his huge body over mine and almost smothers my breathing with his stomach", or "I feel panic when his ejected semen cuts off the air flow in my throat", or "I feel betrayed by one I've been taught to love when pain shoots through me as his large penis tears my small vagina" ?

In the past, it has been common to attempt to deny and avoid the issue of trauma, particularly childhood trauma including physical and sexual abuse. Perhaps the reality of child abuse has been too traumatic for us to face, so our minds, just as the victims' minds, have simply dissociated from the horror, (dissociation defined as failure to integrate normally with existing stored knowledge and perceptions). In addition, perhaps it has been ignored because of so little understanding of problems caused by its effects that victims have to face later in life. Now, however, DEH Russel's *The Secret Trauma, Incest*

In The Lives Of Girls And Women, (among other reports), gives ample evidence to suggest that trauma in childhood is common enough to be a major public health problem.

Sometimes, in a family unit, emotions that are labeled love really aren't. Sometimes the feelings being stimulated are actually sexual feelings. It is common in a hierarchy system to masquerade sexual feelings in the clothing of the label "love." That makes them acceptable. It's done by married men and their vulnerable young mistresses, by priests sexually abusing altar boys and by fathers incesting their children. Most of the time these cases are not reported simply because the victim does not recognize it as criminal activity. The taboo against speaking out about some of the events that cause post traumatic stress is too strong. The Freudian influence of placing the guilt for the action on the victim is too embedded in the system.

It takes tremendous courage for a victim to break the silence. Even though he or she realizes the necessity, and the benefits, of being free from the trauma generated by letting the secret be in control of one's life, the victim also realizes it is a bittersweet victory. Miss America of 1957, Marilyn Van Derbur, has felt both sides of the bittersweet emotions of breaking the silence. As a straight-A student, AAU swimmer, and daughter of a Denver millionaire, the 22-year-old socialite seemed to the public to have a fairy tale life.

It was just that—a fairy tale life. The reality was quite different. She lived in silence with the secret that her father had sexually abused her from the time she was five until she was eighteen. Marrying her high school sweetheart, she continued the fairy tale facade for decades. She paid the price of bouts of paralysis and uncontrollable sobbing. When she could no longer keep up the facade, there was a price to pay. She gained her life, but lost someone she was emotionally bonded with.

When Marilyn made the decision to take back her life it was necessary to break the silence and speak to her parents about being incested. She had to take the consequences of placing her father in a fork in the road. At that point, he would have to choose between two paths (1) take back his own life by breaking the silence, or (2) take the path of avoidance.

The night Marilyn told her parents for the first time that she was seeing a psychiatrist, her father died of a massive heart attack. Her plea to people who recognize symptoms in someone they know who could possibly be a result of childhood trauma is to pick up the phone. Let the person know that you understand that if he or she was abused at age nine it can shut down his or her life at age forty-nine. Assure that you are there to talk to, and that you are a trusted, non-judgmental confident.

When an experience is too painful for us to bear at the moment, our minds protect us from it. The subliminal message is sent: Don't sweat it; avoid or forget it. This is not, nor is it intended to be, a permanent solution. Overflow emotions are only taken off of an overcrowded path and put on a side track for safety as other trains of thought go rushing through. Eventually these thoughts and their feelings, no matter how painful, must get back on the track and finally emerge.

In the end, victims have two choices: continue to try to deny and avoid the pain, or face the demon, experience the pain, and release it. As long as one fights to keep the emotions inside, the emotions fight equally hard to get out. Fighting to keep pain on the side track causes tension generated by inner conflict to accumulate. As long as tension is kept trapped inside, the risk is run that the emotions will choose to suddenly dart out onto the main track and cause a major wreck in our lives. Stress induced illnesses—including heart attacks, gastric problems, psychological amnesia, and flashbacks accompanied by re-enactment of the original trauma—can wreck our lives.

Putting painful experiences on the side track temporarily in order to get strong enough to face them is healthy, but experiences that remain out of the normal flow too long signal an unhealthy situation. The term dissociation is becoming more familiar and easier to understand because of experiences now reported by Vietnam vets. Experiences of overwhelming fear, witnessing friends die, and the excruciating pain of personal injuries were so intolerable to some that their minds split these experiences off and isolated them. The memories are not erased, they are subject to recall when events in the present trigger them. The present is sometimes as unrelated to a war zone as a car backfiring in a local shopping mall parking lot. Dissociation in victims of child abuse follows the same pattern.

A word of caution needs to be included here. Today, people are beginning to respond differently when victims report sexual abuse, even abuse not remembered by the conscious mind for years and years. In the past, people who reported sexual abuse were often looked upon as liars, or crazy, or both. As the stories of more and more people are being checked out and are proven to be true, it is becoming safer for other people to remember long suppressed memories. Confrontation of the traditional silence is resulting in a greater respect for the truth.

However, this opening the floodgate allowing truth to flow out causes a problem for some people who cannot remember their own childhood. It is natural to wonder if the fact that they can't remember is a clue that they, themselves, were sexually abused. NOT ALL PEOPLE WHO CANNOT REMEMBER ANYTHING ABOUT THEIR CHILDHOOD WERE SEXUALLY ABUSED. There are other clues that are worth thinking about: dependency on alcohol, drugs, or relationships, sleep disturbances, eating disorders, promiscuity, workaholism, rigidity or need to control all situations, might be symptoms. Depression in adulthood, particularly in the form of feeling isolated, lonely or different, can be a symptom of having been treated like an object in childhood instead of a person.

Sometimes body memories are triggered by the senses. The smell of toothpaste or Clorox may be associated with the smell of ejaculation. Sometimes an unusual body position can trigger a memory of a sexual act. Repeated waking up panicked in the night at a certain time may be associated with the time of abuse. These things are similar to the flashbacks some Vietnam vets are now having decades after the event. The body remembers even though the mind has suppressed a memory.

Vietnam vets were adults at the time of the trauma. Children experiencing overwhelming fear of dying or suffering intense physical and emotional pain, were not. Their adult verbal abilities or cognitive processes were not yet developed. When adults dissociate and repress traumatic experiences, they tend to store them as complete experiences. When they re-emerge, the whole experience emerges. Children, on the other hand, seem to store them in bits and pieces of feelings and reactions to experiences rather than in complete memories. When the stories re-emerge, they often make little sense to the victims or to people unfamiliar with the aftereffects of childhood trauma.

Children who live through adults' wars are at high risk of living a life of unidentified, free-floating anxiety unless people around them understand the dynamics of trauma. Because their systems are not developed enough to understand war, confusion is a major piece of the fragments of the puzzle they submerge. Often left to draw their own conclusions, these conclusions can be quite distorted. Bubble Babbles can be an important psychological tool to use with children of adults' wars to dislodge memories stored in fragments. Once dislodged and floating on the surface, they can then be connected with arrows in an attempt to identify the train of thought. Bubbles, perhaps represented as balloon on strings, can also double for pressure relief values when needed during painful thoughts. They can be rearranged to follow a logical sequence. As the memory gains structure, it can also be examined for, and adjusted for, reality.

Dr. James A. Chu of Harvard Medical School and McLean Hospital in Belmont, Massachusetts, has studied trauma, dissociation and multiple personality extensively. His work, and his writings, are leading the way for many people to recognize the warning signs in their own lives. His reports are like a pebble dropped in a deep pond covered with a calm surface layer. Although it is not apparent at the surface, much activity is going on at the depths.

With the widening number of people becoming aware of the association between childhood abuse and present-day problems, more and more people are finding the courage to break the surface silence and speak out. This does not have to be done publicly. In fact, in many cases it is counter-productive to speak out publicly. Breaking the silence within a group of supportive peers is an act of courage, and is very stressful for the victim. Using the full force of one's inner energy to fight this initial campaign of the War Against Silence is often a wiser strategy than trying to fight the inner battle and the battle of public reaction at the same time. Speaking out within a group of supportive peers can be a positive healing first step. Until the public becomes more aware of the reality and severity of the devastating aftereffects of childhood trauma, speaking out in public will generate negative energy. As long as the public is uninformed, they will scoff.

Healing is a do-it-yourself project. No one has a responsibility to heal another person. The fact is, no one is able to heal another person. A difference between man and the lower animals is his ability to reason, to make decisions, and to choose. Even after becoming aware of the situation, not all people will choose to exercise their right to heal. Some people find living with aftereffects of a trauma is easier than going through the pain of the healing process, no matter how their behaviors affect people around them.

There comes a time when this reality must be faced. There comes a time when there is a fine line between supporting a person in his or her efforts to heal and enabling a person to continue in the same habits. In this life, behavior has consequences. Consequences must fit the behavior, whether the behavior be efforts to heal or continuation of old behaviors.

There comes a point where what is intended to be support can actually be a shield blocking a person from feeling the consequences of his or her own behavior. In the case of the child abuse cycle, research suggests that in most cases the perpetrator and the abused are both victims. However, there comes a time of accountability for both perpetrator and abused alike. Questions must be asked:

"Is there movement?"

"What stage is the person in—

awareness?
decision?
action?"

Unless there is action, there has been no decision. Our inner guidance system works on movement, not talk *about* movement. Like a torpedo, action propels our life forward until we recognize a mistake. Then our servomechanism corrects the course. Without movement, we sink to the bottom. Without action, we join the ranks of the living dead.

Inherent in this period of accountability is a period of loss, often an unrecognized loss. No matter what the outcome, the helper/victim relationship is obsolete, for it is time to move on. This loss must be grieved. This period of grieving is a period of facing the new reality. This period of healing, or choosing not to heal, clears the field. Either way, there will be a new relationship between the two.

Chapter XIV

ATTACKING THE TRAUMA OF RIGIDITY

(Some names in this chapter changed for privacy)

It's easy to understand how chaotic behavior like incest or alcoholism can cause childhood trauma. Understanding how rigid behavior can cause the same level of dysfunction as chaos is confusing. On the surface, the two lifestyles seem to be on opposite ends of a long, long line. However, on any line from chaos to rigidity, 180 degrees from pain is still pain.

Tim is still reacting to the stimulus of a silent inner dictator replaying messages learned in an extremely rigid childhood. As a young schoolboy attending religious schools of a church based on the hierarchy system, he was at the bottom of the totem pole. As the frustrations of the adults in the hierarchy system were transferred and passed on down the chain of command, he felt the brunt of it—being hit with a ruler for a wrong answer—being forced to write ritual statements of the church twenty-five times when sparks of the creativity that was later to make him successful and famous clashed against the mold of the teachers. I don't know if he had a dog that he could kick when he got home to vent the neuromessengers produced in his body. I do know that parents totally indoctrinated with the rigid beliefs of the church continued the rigidity at home, silencing any questioning of values being passed down to him.

Physically and intellectually, he was able to break out of such abuse. He was born with a beautiful talent which carried him throughout the nation, to foreign countries far from his home town and, eventually, to the very top level of his field. He was not able to break out emotionally. He carried, within his body, an accumulation of stored chemical neuromessengers. These chemicals, like a silent inner dictator, kept stimulating inappropriate reactions of "You're not good enough", "You're going to make a mistake", "You're a pretender."

On top of this inner war, life dumped a real war. Life's not fair. Tim received his orders to go to Vietnam when his wife was pregnant with their third child, and during the construction of a home they thought would be a stable environment for their family. When the family moved into this dream of a home, it was their ninth home in nine years. A time that should have been one of the happiest in this young family's life was, in fact, a time of trauma. The silent, unspoken fear undermining the surface joy of their new family member and new home was "How long will this be a home for a family of five? Will Vietnam make it a home for four?" An inner conflict raged as the brain produced neuromessengers in response to two conflicting stimuli: exciter neuromessengers in response to the joy of a loving family, a new baby, and the fun of building and moving into a new home; inhibitor neuromessengers in response to the fear of loss of a loved one. The brain kept churning out neuromessengers, few of which Tim was able to release. In the rigid society he was raised in, men were taught it was a sign of weakness to talk about, and thereby release, painful emotions. Men were taught to keep a stiff upper lip, submerge painful emotions, and live in silence.

Tim carried this excess baggage of stored neuromessengers with him to Vietnam. Current research shows that he was at higher risk than some to break down emotionally in Vietnam because of this accumulated baggage of emotions, but he didn't. His rigidity, and an apparently highly-efficient opiate system developed over years to protect him from the pain of his culture's abuse, made him a survivor.

The horrors the brain had to protect fighting men from in Vietnam are well known and well documented. There were also dynamics that American fighting men in previous wars had not had to adjust to—the abandonment by their fellow countrymen at home, the questioning by many in their own minds of the morality of the war, and their own self-questioning of the behavior required of them. The speed of modern transportation caused another problem that had not been present in previous wars. This problem is often overlooked. The period of stress debriefing within a support group of peers who had experienced the same horrors during a ten day to several week ocean crossing or land trip back home from wars in the past had been compressed into hours by air travel. Now, with today's speed of modern transportation, there is no time to release emotions that used to be identified and expelled during a ship or land passage. These emotions get shoved under and stored during the excitement of the homecoming.

Often, men stepping off an airplane from Vietnam stepped into a world as emotionally hostile as Vietnam had been physically hostile. They were expected (often required, if they were to survive) to submerge their feelings and carry this excess baggage in silence. Society wanted them to pick up their stateside life where they had left off. Tim did this, and entered a period of accelerated career rise. But, all success contains elements of loss as well as gain. Unless these losses are identified, grieved, and released, the stress from them is added to the accumulated baggage. Still stimulated by thoughts from the silent inner dictator of "You're a pretender", "People will find out what you're really like", "You're not good enough to be this successful", he eventually surrendered the life he and his family had earned—and deserved.

Hierarchy alliances all over the world, whether they be religious, political or social, hold their followers as Hierarchy Hostages. Groups that teach that their thoughts, their behaviors, or their traditions are the only right way hinder people in their life's search for truth—for reality. People raised in an environment of such prejudice are held hostage by that prejudice, no matter what level on the hierarchy pole they happen to be at the moment. The walls of the prison of restricted thinking of a New York socialite can be just as strong, and just as emotionally injurious, as the barriers around that same city's minority prisoners of prejudice.

In a hierarchy system, somebody's way has to be right; somebody's way has to be wrong. Somebody has to be good; somebody has to be bad. Somebody has to be higher; somebody has to be lower. Somebody has to be controller; somebody has to be controlled. Control comes in many guises, some so subtle it is not easily recognized as control. Its manipulation is often masked as "love." Often, the balance between love and manipulation to fill the controller's own needs is so close it tips back and forth depending on the situation. A good person can do bad things. There is a difference between what a person is and what a person does. It is important to understand this, and to be able to separate in one's mind what a person is and what a person does in different situations.

On a deeper level, the right/wrong, good/bad, higher/lower, controller/controlled attitude translates into self-image. A person can come to believe "If I am the one who is right, I have a right to say who can live." In an hierarchy system, the one who is higher has the power to control the lives and moods of the one who is lower. People who are lower often become dependent personalities, choosing to give away their own personal power in exchange for having their physical or emotional needs taken care of by others. However, power can be abused. The controller's hand that pats a dependent person on the head in approval can change into one with a finger being shaken in disapproval. As an extension of an inner attitude which grows in intensity, a finger being shaken in disapproval can progress to a hand slapping a face, then to a fist holding a gun. Hitler was an hierachist with a gun in his hand.

Just a few weeks before the break-up of the Soviet Union, Julia Gippenreiper, then a professor of psychology at Moscow University in the Soviet Union and author of seven books on the topic, talked with me about her memories.

JULIA: I remember my feeling of pride standing on a stage with other children my age when I was seven, singing about the teachings and accomplishments of Joseph Stalin. As a child, I was taught these beliefs and taught to be a model to help others learn them. I recall how proud I was to be a part of such a wonderful country. On the other hand, I also remember incidences where friends and relatives simply dropped out of sight. Adults refused to answer questions or even discuss these disappearances at all. This part of my childhood was treated as a big secret. I was warned not to discuss any of it with anybody. No one was to be trusted with details of events in the area of the "big secret." As a child, I kept the adults' secret, but I didn't know what it was.

In time, as hints began to emerge that Stalin was orchestrating both of these areas of my life, (my beliefs and the disappearances of friends), I felt confusion and disbelief. I couldn't integrate the information that I, as an intelligent person, was now realizing. As more and more proof surfaced and I could no longer deny it, I felt betrayed and angered. Confusion, then sadness over my loss of identity, followed. I asked myself "If I am not, as I have always thought, a supporter of a noble cause, who am I?" When I finally faced the reality that the beliefs I had been taught as a child by people and institutions I trusted were not true I, like anyone experiencing a disillusionment, had decisions to make.

What I see in my clients today mirrors the choices I had. There is a wide range of choices for how to cope with disillusionment. The healthier the choice a person picks, the happier the future life built on a foundation of that choice will be. As a person grows healthier emotionally, he or she can choose to replace choices that cause painful consequences with healthier ones. I see my countrymen picking from a range of choices for coping with economic and social problems.

Outlining choices from pessimistic to optimistic, some choose **DENIAL,** looking for bad features of this transition time and yearning for a time of order. People find it hard to cope with chaos and say "At least then there was order; at least then there was bread." The next type of reaction is a sense of **LOSS OF SELF**. People think: What shall we do? That world is gone where I knew my future, where I knew what my options were. They see no direction for the future. The structure of social life they have known has disappeared and their identity has been lost. They ask "Who am I if I am not who I have always believed I was?" The next kind of reaction is that of people who say **"OH, A BREATH OF FRESH AIR, OR POSSIBILITIES**" These people say "Yes, I used to do one thing, but now that isn't working and I am not satisfied. I have other choices now. Maybe I will explore my new possibilities."

People on the next level get past the hesitation. They don't say "Maybe I'll do it." Rather, they say "I'll do it now." They say "I feel it is my responsibility to change, at least this small part of the world." They begin to be active in their field in new ways. In my country now, these people may start their own businesses, an opportunity just recently opened for them.

Another group of people, similar to these people but actually a different type, look with a broader vision than just to start a business or do different things in one field. People at this level are the leaders and architects of their new world. They think, plan and discuss new ways for the country, new routes to take. There are a lot of articles in our magazines now discussing which way our country should choose. In the past, we have been bound to follow Slavic traditions. Now, people are discussing different ways of thinking. With the type of people who choose the more optimistic choices, feelings are not depressive. They are full of life; they see the opportunities and feel hope for the future. I see myself as part of the fifth group, people who choose to **CHANGE THEMSELVES AND THEIR SOCIETY BY TAKING ACTION.** Following this approach, several of my colleagues and I joined energies several years ago to form the Institute for Humanistic Relations and Personal Growth in Moscow. Recent profound changes had put my country into a time of transition. Although there have always been problems, people were never allowed to discuss them openly. The new openness of Glasnost give people not used to having their politicians debate these problems in newspapers a general feeling of anxiety. The relaxation of rigidity had also led to a rise in the crime rate. People were afraid. There were many people looking for help, but there were few therapists. In the 1930's, Stalin's policies repressed the work of psychotherapists and it was not until the 1970's that they could freely practice again. Students being trained now have few older, experienced professionals to model or work under to get practical experience. One of the Institute's projects is bringing teams of therapists from the United States to conduct workshops in Russia. We asked Maureen and Tom Graves of the New Hope Alcohol and Addiction Center in South Sioux City, Nebraska, to lead a section on alcoholism because they have extensive experience training others.

TOM: Alcoholism is considered a very serious problem with people in Julia's country—some estimates run as high as one in three. I observed that families' living arrangements contribute to the problem. There is not enough housing for each family to have its own space. With so little privacy, interaction with outsiders in one's home is almost impossible. Because sports, eating, and drinking are the major ways to make contact outside the home, alcohol plays an important part in the culture.

MAUREEN: I think a lot of the symptoms of post traumatic stress I saw result from living in a rigid, dysfunctional system. This system mirrors the family environment many abused children or children of dysfunctional families grow up in our country. As adults, a dark cloud hangs over some because, even though they are supposed to be free and out of that system now, they still live in the same fear of an attack. This is a major symptom of post traumatic stress. For example, one man told me his reaction to talking to a friend about not liking what the government was doing with sugar. He said that after he got off the phone he was struck with the thought: The KGB could be at my door at any minute. He said "I couldn't shake that feeling. It was there about a week." Even though the trauma is supposedly over, the post traumatic stress effects are still there. Another symptom I saw prominently was suppressed grief. Because people didn't consciously realize what was happening at the time, fear and grief was repressed and is still stored inside. When we live with a fear but don't really recognize it because our conscious mind is telling us "This is good" "This is a wonderful country" "This is a wonderful family I live in", we have the fear inside us but it never gets out. Until this stress is identified, expressed, and released, there is an inner conflict due to lack of harmony between what our conscious mind is telling us and what our body chemicals are stimulating. I saw this free-floating anxiety in some people. I see the same symptoms in my clients here who are not able to talk about how it was to live in fears generated, but unidentified, while growing up in a dysfunctional family.

This is what our work as therapists is all about. Because we realize that it is important, we work to help people identify and release emotions after a trauma—including the trauma of being raised in an excessively rigid country or family.

Chapter XV

I FOUGHT A BATTLE IN STRANGE TERRITORY

By the time I finished writing the article, my editor Carol and I knew it was not right for the magazine. By then we realized that the problem was far too complex to be developed in a limited number of pages. I sent it to the magazine's editor anyway because he had been so helpful and supportive that I did not want him to think I had not taken the project seriously. His comments affirmed what Carol and I already knew. He was very encouraging and, in the end, the article grew into a book. This made it a much more complicated project. At this point I realized I had to do it on a professional basis or not at all. The information was much too important for an avocation approach.

Time came to make a decision to continue the project or drop it. By the deadline to sign up to exhibit the new book at the American Booksellers' Association Convention seven months away, I simply didn't know what to do. Again I communed. "If I'm meant to write this book I will, but you have to find the financing because I'm broke. Please send me a sign."

The very next day, as I was driving down my street, I saw a garage sale sign in front of one of the old Victorian houses that line it. I always check out garage sales in old Victorian houses because that is about the only place I can find fixtures, fittings, and woodwork that I need in the restoration of my home. I whizzed around the block and pulled up in front of the carriage house. The wife was not at home at the moment;

the husband was running the garage sale. He and I chatted as I poked around, ooed and ahhed, and bought a few things. When I told him I was an author he said

RAY: What type of books do you write?

EMILY: Well, the last one I wrote was on the crash of Flight 232 here in town. This one is an outgrowth of that. It's about Post-Traumatic Stress but not just from airplane crashes or Viet Nam. A lot of other traumas cause Post-Traumatic Stress too, but most people don't realize that yet and don't recognize the symptoms. But, I don't know if it's going to get printed because I'm broke. What I need is a Sugar Daddy.

He continued to ask questions as I continued to poke around. When he finished helping me load the back of my station wagon, he closed it down and asked.

RAY: How much would it cost to publish that book?

EMILY: I don't know. Haven't made up the budget yet.

RAY: When you do, come to see me. That's what I do.

EMILY: WHAT do you do? (I had just told this man I needed a Sugar Daddy.)

RAY: I'm a stock broker, but some of my clients are interested in that type of investment.

I thought: Okay—there is no way that I, or anybody else, could misread what has just happened. This is obviously my sign. I have no doubt that I am being told to go ahead with the project. So, having made the commitment to exhibit the book, I set about full force working on it.

With the piece of the puzzle of the possibility of funding having fallen into place, the whole mood of the project changed. I realized I had to restructure the project on a business basis. The problem was I did not know anything about a business basis. I needed some more Satellite Staff. Some years ago, I had won two Department of Energy national competitions for Solar Energy Design. There had been a lady at the Small Business Administration, Rosemary Mullany, who had been very supportive and helpful to me with my project at that time.

Problem was, I hadn't talked to her in about ten years and didn't know where she worked now. I did remember the name of a man I thought was a friend of hers at SBA years ago, so I called a government office and asked a friend if she knew of him. She found his number. I called it and he answered the phone. I asked him if knew Rosie's phone number, but he didn't remember her.

EMILY: I thought you knew her at SBA and you both moved to the Commerce Department when the Administration was broken up.

SHERMAN: That was ten years ago. I've worked two places since the SBA. Give me your name and your friend's name though. I'll see if I can find her.

Two days later I got a call from Rosie.

ROSIE: Emily! I just got a call from a lady who works for the Inspector General of the United States saying to call Emily. WHAT HAVE YOU DONE?

EMILY: So I told her I had written a book and . . .

ROSIE: WHY IS THE INSPECTOR GENERAL IN ON THIS?

EMILY: I didn't know he was the Inspector General until you just told me. All I knew was I thought he was a friend of yours.

ROSIE: He was the Director of the SBA before they did away with it. I was an employee there. That's not what you'd call friends. You remember the name because I booked the two of you as panelists on a program, but you never met him because the event was canceled.

EMILY: Oh. (When things get beyond what I can handle, I often just go into the Oh-zone.)

Rosie is now Director of Women's Business Programs at the Commerce Department. After talking to her, I called Dennis Bogenrief at the Small Business Development Center here in Sioux City. With his help, I learned how to draw up a business proposal and budget. When I finished it, I took it to Ray. It was four weeks before Ray called me back.

Looking at the figures on paper as I drew up the plan, I felt the weight of responsibility. I became very methodical and much more serious in my research. I became driven and far too intense. For the next year, this project totally consumed my life. I wrote; I worked closely with Dennis to learn the business end of it; I wrote; I spent hours in research libraries; I wrote; I took interview trips; I wrote; I took promotion trips; and I wrote.

The warmth Kathe Perle and her staff at St. Lukes' Hospital Instructional Center enveloped me in when I walked in gave a balance to the chill I felt at some of the information I was reading in the magazines and books there. The hospital's chaplain, Rudy Oudheusden, had just recently died. At the time of his death he had been working on a magazine article about Post Traumatic Stress. The staff was eager to help continue work on the topic out of respect to him and because they understood the importance of the research he had been finding. They were aware of the seriousness of the problem, and also of how little was known about it yet.

I could always count on a cheerful "How can I help you?" greeting from Sister Bernice Schuetz, Library Director of Briar Cliff College, when I walked in. She, her helpful staff, and the airiness and spaciousness of the library, lifted my spirits. The wonderful people at the Reference Desk at the Sioux City Library often had answers for me to questions I hadn't even asked. They get a lot of calls for information about the crash and its victims, and often realized points I should be considering that I hadn't thought of. Kim Browne there put together an index of all the articles about the crash published in the Sioux City Journal newspaper. I found it very helpful, and know researchers will be benefiting from it for years to come. Leo Kriz knew how to identify the right areas so people could find the book among so many in a library when it was finished.

Some of the most important research I was finding was by an epidemiologist in Michigan. I didn't know exactly what an epidemiologist was. I thought I remembered hearing a friend of mine use that word in years past. I hadn't seen Margaret, alias Gigi, in over thirty years. I was a guest in her parents' home when she was married and she, her husband and I visited back and forth for a few years after. I then lost contact with her until the book *Souls On Board* came out. When an order for a book for her and each one of her six children came in, the friendship was immediately renewed. Authors feels a close friendship with people who buy seven books, even people they haven't met before. I called her.

EMILY: Didn't you use word epidemiology when we were talking once? Do you know what epidemiology is?

GIGI: Of course I know what epidemiology is. It pays for my house and groceries. My husband is the State Epidemiologist of Michigan.

EMILY: Oh.

GIGI: Norm's here. Let me get him on the other phone.

I told them about my project and about the research being done in Detroit that I was finding so helpful. Norm knew the lady I was referring to, Naomi Breslau, and had worked with her father, also an epidemiologist. In hindsight, what happened next blows my mind.

NORM: There's always room in our home for someone with a project as exciting as yours. Why don't you come to Michigan, plug your computer in at our house, and write your manuscript here?

EMILY: (Thinking back, considering I hadn't seen these people for over thirty years, I find my answer unbelievable.) I can't come today. The symphony's Saturday.

NORM: Then come Sunday.

EMILY: I can't come Sunday. I'm editor of the Symphony Guild newsletter and I made a big mistake on the last issue. I have to re-do them and send them out again.

NORM: How many?

EMILY: 350

NORM: No, you can't come Sunday, but do come when you can.

I redid the newsletter, sent it out, rented a computer, and packed up to go to Michigan. In the meantime, I called Charlene, another friend from years and years ago, who works in the public relations field in Detroit. I told her about my project and what had happened.

CHARLENE: Oh, that sounds just like what our friend John talks about all the time. You remember John. The three couples of us used to be such good friends in Texas. He'll be happy to help you. John's now head of the Department of Psychopharmacology at the University of Michigan. We'll get together when you come.

Well, I didn't remember much about "our friend John", nor he about me, but we both took Charlene's word for it. It had been twenty-five years since we'd all been together in Texas.

I was all packed up and ready to go to Michigan when Ray called and told me to come down to his office. I'd planned to leave the following morning, Thanksgiving Day. Mario, my son who lives about six hours away, was to put a turkey in the oven when I left. We'd take it out when I got there and have a family Thanksgiving dinner. Now, an alert was out warning anybody planning to travel for Thanksgiving to leave right away. A major ice storm was coming and the roads would probably be closed the next day.

RAY: I want you to come down to my office right away. I've found a client who is interested in your project. He's flying in to Sioux City from Los Angeles and the three of us will get together and discuss it. You need to do some work on this proposal first. Come down so we can talk about it.

I thought: This is nuts. I have to get on the highway before the roads ice over. But, because of the importance of it, I stopped at his office. My business plan wasn't very business-like. It took him a while to explain how I needed to change it.

RAY: (as a closing remark) And Emily, when a man invests his money in the creativity of your mind, he's not called a Sugar Daddy. He's called an investor. As a business point, I suggest you start using that word.

I went home . . . grabbed as many of the related financial files as I could think of in such a hurry, . . . noticed I had an almost entirely flat tire on the car, . . . stopped and had it changed . . . and took off as it was getting dark.

The weather report was accurate. Anybody who waited until Thanksgiving morning to try to take off was icebound. People couldn't even get from their homes to the airport. Mario and I had a lovely Thanksgiving dinner and gave thanks that I was in Cedar Rapids instead of Sioux City. Problem was I couldn't get out of Cedar Rapids the next day, or the next, or the next. That worked out okay because Gigi and Norm wouldn't have been home to let me in if I had. They were icebound where they had gone for Thanksgiving dinner.

Since I had promised Ray I would come home immediately when the investor let him know he was coming into town, I now had to divide my time between working on the manuscript and revising the proposal. Norm helped me set up my computer in a private bedroom where I could continue my pattern of writing from four until noon. He has a critical eye of a medical scientific investigator. He saw that my Bubble Babble writing followed a predictable pattern. Starting from the circle around the first thought that came to my mind in the morning, my thoughts began by radiating in many directions. Sometimes the taped pages had to be spread out on the floor because they followed so many different lines of thought. Norm pointed out that, at first, so many thoughts hit me at once that it looked like total confusion. It wasn't. The trains of thought could easily be followed by following the arrows.

Some days the explosive activity went on for a long time; other days it settled down much sooner. The writing eventually became linear, with one thought flowing from another without distracting thoughts shooting off on a tangent of circles. Norm pointed out that it was as if I had to clear my head of many thoughts before I could concentrate on one. By writing them in bubbles, the important ones could easily be seen. The lesser ones could be developed at a later time.

Gigi doesn't like to cook; she's cooked out after raising six kids. I like to cook and enjoyed planning, walking through the snow to get groceries, and cooking many of the evening meals. After supper, she and I'd sit in front of the fireplace feeling the warmth of both the fire and our friendship.

I was also able to visit Charlene and Dave in the beautiful historic home they are restoring in Brighton. They've remodeled the kitchen so she doesn't miss out on any of the action when she's preparing a meal. I suppose it is not quite historically accurate for a house as formal as theirs, which obviously needed a whole staff of servants to run. But, it's a lot of fun for hosts and guests to sit in the kitchen then help carry the food to the dining room. On another day, Charlene took me to lunch in the dining room of the corporate headquarters where she works. As I walked across the parking lot on my way to meet her, I thought: We've come a long way baby! The trappings had changed dramatically since we'd been friends as young wives living in apartments with three sons each twenty-five years ago, but we were the same kids at heart.

While with Gigi and Norm, I learned a lot about how my self-image controls my moods and behavior. An incident one afternoon was convincing evidence of how my mind can damn me to purgatory with a single emotion—fear. We walked down to the business area of town and had a lovely Sunday afternoon—at least on the surface. Went into a bookstore designed for browsing—free coffee, round oak tables with chairs, a kiddie play area built like a fort with toys inside, and bins of out-of-town Sunday newspapers for sale. We sat with coffee and newspapers for a while, then began to browse through the store. Suddenly, negative thoughts began to ambush me. By the time I left that store I felt like a total failure, even though no one had said an unkind word to me. A parade of thoughts admonished: "I can't take the risk of getting the money from that investor. I will fail." "I'm not good enough to pull this off." "I will lose my home if I go into debt." "I'm an impostor coming here to Michigan as a writer." "I'm imposing on Gigi and Norm because I'm here under false pretenses pretending to be a real writer."

In hindsight, I realize it began when we reached the new book section of the store. First I noticed the size of the books. I thought "My book will never sell because it's not big enough." (This in spite of the fact that it had already sold out of the first printing.) The next fearful thought was "My book will never sell because I can't get these high-powered endorsements." Then, of course, I thought "If it is a success I will still fail because I will make a fool of myself on radio and TV interviews." Thoughts fed to me by my negative self-image kept up until I was totally panicked by the time we left the store. This all took place on the inside. Talking about it later, Gigi and Norm said they had no clue my public image and my self image were battling it out and destroying me. I now know, thought I didn't then, that toxic chemicals produced by internal battles like these can cause gastric or digestive problems. Until demons from experiences and trainings in the past are acknowledged, faced and released, they fight viscously to get out. When we do not allow it through normal channels, they can come out in another form such as psychosomatic illness.

Soon, a crisis in my family distracted my thoughts to the point that I could no longer write. Creative writing is not like many other types of work. Not only is concentration necessary but, in addition, there is a little child that has to bounce around, giggle at new thoughts that bubble up and think "Hey I should write that down." Now, my little child was distracted, . . . and sad. With Christmas getting near and a son coming home for the holidays, I left. I told Gigi and Norm I could come back later but it just wasn't any use for me to stay to write any more. I wouldn't be able to do justice to the interviews.

After Christmas, emotions began to build in our community as the date neared for televising of the film about the rescue efforts after the crash, *Crash Landing: The Rescue of Flight 232,* staring Charlton Heston as the pilot, James Coburn as Sioux Gateway Airport Fire Chief and Richard Thomas as the Woodbury County Disaster Services Director. Due to the subject of the movie, a conscious effort was made to downplay the Hollywood hoopla. Instead, the emphasis was placed on community cooperation. The movie was dedicated to "those who died, those who survived, and those who prepared."

The movie captures on film the caring spirit of the community and illustrates a strong belief of mine. Being prepared for an accident is no accident. It is the consequence of behavior, the behavior of preparing. The community's response to the United Flight 232 tragedy was an automatic response to the city's ecology, it's relationship between plants, animals and people. As an agricultural community, people live with and are comfortable with the natural cycle of life—a time to start, a time to grow, and a time to die. Because they are comfortable with it, they don't look away to avoid thinking about a time to die.

The movie is one more tile in the mosaic that is being developed for history. What happened that day cannot be recorded on one smooth brush sweep of a unified picture. It is a collection of tiles of stories of human individuals, of a community effort of people pulling together. It showcases an ecology based on human values that are more important than financial or political status. It's a fluid picture, changing and growing as the lives of the people involved continue.

There is life after death on this earth. Those who are left grieve, but they still live—at least biologically. Grief is a process. It is not a state of existence. Eventually, experiences in the present act as a challenge to the trauma and a call to action in the present. After a trauma, the mind protects us from feeling too much pain with immobilizing shock that causes inability to act. Eventually, however, a person must reach the stage to take action again in order to get over the emotions after the trauma.

The community went through the process of lancing the boil together in several steps. When a boil is lanced, not all of the puss oozes out at one time. The first lancing came at the time of the one year anniversary memorial service. Much healing took place then. Later, painful emotions rose to the surface during the filming of the movie as incidences of the day were reenacted. The filming was an emotional time for the actors too. Charlton Heston, who played Capt. Al Haynes, spoke about his feelings when he was back in Sioux City for the premier of the film. He said it emotionally touched him to see people who were not performers standing there with tears in their eyes as the cameras were rolling on those reenacting the scenes of what they did that day. The movie is a story of human beings being put to a test outside of the realm of their normal life. This is listed as one of the criterias of Post Traumatic Stress listed in the Physician's Diagnostic Manual. Going over the experience in such a realistic way was therapeutic for survivors and rescue workers who had small parts. It brought emotions to the surface that had been stuck. Healing took place when, once to the surface, they could be faced and released.

The experience in the present was laced with incidences of comic relief. The experience July 19, 1989, was not. The very cornfield where many of the survivors landed provided its own story of comic relief. Filming was to be done in the summer, the season the crash occurred. As anybody who saw pictures of the flaming ball of fire rolling across the Iowa cornfield so vividly captured by Dave Boxom of KTIV-Channel 4 in Sioux City knows, no one who was there at the time had any reason to believe that there were survivors. The Emergency First Responders began their work thinking there were not. Much to everyone's surprise, after a period of time people began walking out of the cornfield. The corn was so high it had screened them from view until they actually reached the edge of the field.

As the schedule for filming dragged out, the season changed. The beautiful green corn turned brown. This presented a serious problem and called for creative thinking. The crew painted the corn green. That night it rained and the corn turned brown again. They painted it green again and, amid much laughter, filmed quickly. All was well.

Time passed, and the seasons changed again. The premier showing was in the winter. Again, stored emotions began rising to the surface. This time they were from two experiences: the experience of the actual crash, and the experience of the filming of the crash. In some cases, the two sets of emotions conflicted. People approached the premier, the facing of the harvest of the fruit of their labors, carrying the baggage of their emotions in response to what they knew they had done. Some felt only pride for their behavior and their contribution to the film. Others did not. This was another lancing of the boil as emotions, both negative and positive, spewed out all over the community.

Some people were hurt when everyone didn't get equal recognition following the crash. There were hard feelings then, and these hard feelings resurfaced again at the time of the showing of the movie. The film was not a documentary; some serious liberties were taken with the facts. The one that caused the most negative reaction in the community was the fictional friction written in between the Director of the County Disaster Services and the Sioux Gateway Airport Fire Chief. James Coburn's character is portrayed as a man resistant to change fighting against Richard Thomas' to keep the "old way" of doing things. In real life, Gary is quick to point out that he and Jim Hathaway are friends and that Jim has always been an advocate of disaster preparedness. "We've gotten along ever since I can remember. Jim was one of the big players to get our disaster committee put together." There was turf fighting in the first hour or so of the crisis until Governor Brandstad made clear the chain of authority in our state, but it wasn't between these two men.

The nationwide showing of the film stirred up renewed interest in the book *Souls On Board: Responses to the United Flight 232 Tragedy*. I was asked to do many interviews. These experiences made me realize that I did not know how to handle interviews very well, and that I again needed additional skill training.

Before the scheduled time for my first interview, I took great pains to prepare in order to be ready. I decided that the most private spot would be at the phone next to my bed, in a turret high on the third floor of my home. I spread reference papers and notes all over my bed. They were taped up the curved walls of the turret running right around the edges of my bed. I could see them clearly as I was sitting in my bed. The telephone rang right at the time it was scheduled to and the interview began. It was with a major news service and the host was in San Diego, California. Pretty soon my call-waiting beeper beeped, but I knew this was important so I didn't answer it. It kept beeping.

HOST: Is that your line beeping?

EMILY: Yes, but I'm ignoring it.

HOST: Well, you can't ignore it when you're on national radio. Answer it. I can't interview you with the beeper beeping.

So, I put him on hold and answered it. It was a lady in town who had read in the paper that I had written a book and wanted to talk to me about a book she had written. She wanted to ask how to get it published. I told her I couldn't talk to her right then as I was giving a radio interview, and I went back to the other line. We started again, and my beeper started again.

HOST: Answer it.

I answered it. It was the producer of the Jenny Jones show. I told her I couldn't talk to her right then as I was giving an interview on the other line and asked if she would call back in about a half hour. I was so inexperienced that I did not realize that this was not the answer to give to a producer of a syndicated television show. She was nice enough, however, to call back. By this time the radio host was understandably irritated and the questions from then on were rather hostile. I was glad when the interview was over, and I'm sure he was too.

The next interview was scheduled at 7 o'clock in the morning my time, 8 o'clock Florida time where the host was. Five minutes before the scheduled time, the telephone rang and the technician went through the preliminaries, then told me he was going to put me on hold. The next I heard was the dial tone. I hung up so there would be no busy signal on my end and pretty soon a very frustrated technician called back and reconnected me. But, by this time the host was thinking in the next time slot and so was calling me by the wrong name and asking me questions meant for the person who was to be interviewed after me. He did a wonderful job of recovery when someone obviously told him his mistake however, and from that point on the interview went smoothly.

The most electrifying experience I had came during an interview with a host in Philadelphia, the city that had been the destination of Flight 232. This was a three-way interview between host Bernie Herman in Philadelphia, Captain Haynes in Seattle, and me in my bed in my turret in Sioux City. There was a terrible thunder storm raging outside. At one point during the interview, Capt. Haynes was talking about the huge ball of fire and flames surrounding the airplane after it crashed. All of a sudden through my curved turret windows, which I had never before noticed are very suggestive of curved cockpit windows, all I could see were flames shooting up and completely covering my view outside the window. I thought "Holy Cow! This turret's gonna crash!"

Then everything went dark. I couldn't see anything down the street from out of the window except darkness. I fought to stay calm, and completed the interview. It was an hour long interview with listener call-in at the end. Afterwards, I found out that lightening had struck my house. I did not find out until the following day that it had then traveled along the electric wire to the back of the house. Karen, one of the ladies who lived in my home, was standing in the kitchen, saw the ball of flame come in, and saw it travel down the edge of the stove. I was very lucky. There are two lines on that same pole. I was fortunate that it traveled along the electric line rather than along the telephone wire and into my ear.

The next day a man from Chadds Ford, Pennsylvania, who had grown up in Sioux City, called and introduced himself. When I told him what had happened he said that his granddaughter had taped the interview and that he would check it. He said he didn't remember having any hint that anything was wrong on my end. After he checked the tape, he called back and told me that there was no sign in my voice of what had happened. He sent me a copy of the tape. When he and his wife came back for his 50th high school reunion, he and another couple they had gone to high school with took me out to lunch. Meeting wonderful people is one of the perks of being an author.

During an interview with a host in Detroit, one of the listeners who called in mentioned the effort Capt. Haynes makes to help survivors work through their emotions. She explained how he goes out of his way to contact them and share his compassion. So, next time I talked to him, I told him the struggle Pam was having with her emotions.

EMILY: Al, because she moved away from Sioux City, she's living in a town where she knows no one who went through the experience and can understand what really went on here that day.

AL: Let me look at my schedule. I think I'm supposed to give a speech in Colorado Springs soon. Yes, I'm scheduled for April.

I know that speakers don't have much time to themselves in towns where they speak. The schedule is usually pretty full. I was surprised to learn later that he and his host, the Fire Chief of Colorado Springs, spent a lot of time the afternoon of his speech trying to help a lady who they knew needed help. First they tried to find Pam's phone number but couldn't. Al knew that she worked at the Air Force Academy Hospital, so they went there, but she wasn't at work that day. They got her phone number, but she wasn't home either. They never were able to make contact with her that day. That night, however, she was in the audience. She went up and introduced herself afterwards. Al took her to the side and talked privately with her right there. She went away feeling not so alone in her grief as when she had come. She felt connected.

Al spends a lot of time since the accident helping people understand the ace in the hole he is using to deal with his emotions after the trauma:

A - awareness
C - connection
E - experiences in the present.

Chapter XVI

OVERTHROWING THE SILENT INNER DICTATOR

I realized that this was another point in my life where my opportunities had pulled ahead of my knowledge. In order to give them my best shot I had to get additional training. I discussed it with Joni Wilde, my assistant. As usual, her advice was "You just go and don't worry about anything here. I'll take care of everything here." I called Dottie Walters, author of the book *Speak and Grow Rich,* made arrangements to attend one of the seminars she holds in her home and off I flew to California.

On the plane, I did a lot of thinking about how different life is now than when I was in college for the first time over thirty years ago. The thinking at that time was that one prepared for a career, (men working outside the home, women working in the home), worked at that career, and then retired into leisure activities. It was all very linear. Life isn't like that any more. My thinking is that it changed because of the advances in medicine and health. Now, when people reach retirement age and their kids are gone they live longer, feel better, still have a lot of energy, and don't feel like sitting on a porch in a rocking chair for too long at a time.

Our culture has changed. Now, people train in an area of interest, work in that area and, as they learn more about it, see new opportunities they don't have the training for. So, they train in that new area of interest, work in that new area, etc., etc., etc. Just as before, work still has beginnings and endings but now, because of extended life span and better health, people can fit more of these cycles in. I knew that my life was having a new beginning now. But, unlike I thought I could when I was a young adult, I could not predict what the ending would be.

We landed in California and I rented a car. This was a new experience for me. In the culture I had lived in, renting a car was definitely men's work, as was driving in California freeway traffic. I took back roads to the motel.

Dottie, her husband Cowboy Bob, and daughter Lillie, (who is also a speaker), took me out to dinner. I really appreciated that because it gave me the opportunity to ease into the unknown area of big-time speakers. It gave me the chance to find out that they were just as human as little time speakers. Then home to the motel, and Cowboy Bob told me he'd pick me up the next morning. That's the last I saw of Cowboy Bob. The next morning plans were changed and he went to the airport to pick up another attendee. Someone else picked me up. That day I learned a lot more than what Dottie had on her agenda at the start of the day. I also learned about total professionalism.

About ten of us sat around the fireplace in her downstairs office drinking coffee, munching on sweetbreads, and getting acquainted. Then we went into her conference room and the flow of information started. About mid morning, Lillie stuck her head in the door at the back of the room.

LILLIE: Mom, Dad slipped on a wet spot at the post office. He hurt his leg and some people took him to the hospital but he said to tell you don't worry about it, he's okay.

Don't worry about it? I had spent the evening with this family the night before. I had seen, and been included in, the tight bond of caring between them. Cowboy Bob had a similar problem with his leg several years before, a painful, long ordeal. This woman must be exploding inside. She acknowledged Lillie and continued on with the presentation just as if her whole life had not drastically changed with that remark. A sensitive lady in the room called out

CAROLYN: Dottie, why don't we take an early lunch and you can go see your husband in the hospital?

The group immediately chimed in and assured her that this was what we would like her to do. I sought out the lady to go to lunch with. She proved to be as interesting as she was compassionate, and I felt an instant friendship with her. After lunch, we went back and Dottie picked up where she left off. In the afternoon, Lillie again stuck her head in the back door.

LILLIE: Mom, the doctors have decided they have to do surgery and they've taken Dad to the operating room, but he said he's all right and for you not to worry.

Dottie acknowledged her remark but never missed a beat in her presentation. I learned a lot from that grand lady that day. I was scheduled to have a private session with her the next day, but I was going to be in California for a while so I suggested we postpone it. I suggested she call me and reschedule it when she knew more about how her husband's condition. She seemed to appreciate the freedom. We met later.

While I was in California I interviewed Liz, an adult who grew up in a dysfunctional family. (To protect her privacy, I'm not using her real name.) Adults who grew up as children in dysfunctional families or societies almost invariably live with a silent partner, an inner dictator sending them subliminal messages of survival. Liz, an outwardly successful workaholic, compulsively conquered each theater in her career crusade. Her campaign was flawless. She invaded classroom after accredited college classroom and analyzed each job offer or promotion. She still does. She also has migraine headaches.

Problem is, her subliminal messages of survival are out of date. Because they are subliminal, they are silent. Even though she does not have access to them on the conscious level, they control her life. This inner conflict, between outdated subliminal survival commands and present day reality, gives her migraine headaches.

Our perceptions stimulate production of chemicals. It is what we perceive a person, place or thing to be (not what they really are) that determines what type of transmitter is produced. Scientist have now discovered that neuromessengers are not confined to the brain area. They travel through our whole bodies, like hormones do, doing their work.

We live, and raise our children if we have any, by the rules we were taught when we were children. Until the taboo against questioning the reality of the teachings of our parents or society began to be lifted a bit recently, there was no other place to learn parenting techniques. Now there is, and oftentimes what we learn is that the survival rules we were taught (verbally or non-verbally) are outdated . . . they no longer work. Often, we also learn that they were abusive. That second lesson is a particularly hard one to learn, and a hard one to process after we learn it. Understanding something intellectually and being able to absorb it and process it so that it becomes part of the pathway our thinking runs over are two different things.

However, there can be no inner peace until the battle subsides between the silent survival rules we needed as children and the rules of our present day reality. A general must be found to lead the campaign, a gentle general whose battle cry is LET'S TALK! I care about you. Because of the dynamics of trauma, our opiate system will not allow us to fight this war alone. We need feedback from someone who is not opiated from the reality of the cause of our personal pain.

Liz gets feedback. This feedback is based on reality. She made the decision and, more importantly, took the action to get professional help. Liz enlisted the help of a therapist and MD who trained her to recognize the signals of an approaching migraine attack and give her prescriptions for external chemicals to blunt it. She has, however, an unseen enemy in her war. Her perception of reality (which is not the same thing as reality) and her Silent Dictator's perception of reality were formed within the framework of the teachings of a church whose teachings dictate that no external medicinal chemicals should be taken into the body. In Liz, the warning signs of an approaching migraine attack apparently trigger an additional stress of a battle between her Silent Dictator's perception of reality and her perception and new awareness of the necessity to take the medicine to conquer the on-coming assault to her body.

Now, after not having seen Liz for five years, business took me to her city at a time when I was able to schedule an entire week of solitary writing. For me, a relatively unstructured period like this usually proves to be a nurture Emily break. I was on an extremely tight deadline to get this manuscript finished and the interviews I needed were with people far from my Iowa home. I checked into a beautiful condominium with a cozy fireplace, large expanses of windows and several balconies overlooking calming Pacific Ocean vistas. Liz and I were excited at the prospect of a reunion. We made plans to meet for church on Sunday (though not the church of the religion she had been raised in), then grill steaks on a balcony looking down on a green expanse dotted with flowering trees to where whitecaps broke on rocks on the wide beach.

Friday was an extremely stressful work day for her and, in hindsight, she remembers experiencing the warning signs of an approaching migraine attack. Apparently, her Silent Dictator won the fight that time because she took no action. Perhaps an over-active opiate system strengthened through many experiences of numbing her from pain anesthetized her again and numbed her ability to process the warning signals.

The battle lasted two days. Saturday, my workaholic friend missed college training that was important to her and Sunday she missed a special day of relaxing and self-nurturing that she deserved. Instead, she was held hostage in her own bedroom and bath suffering pain and throwing up.

Silent Dictators must be defeated before we can speak out and win the war against the silence resulting from subliminal thought pathways. These pathways, grooved by former experiences, make no sound. However, they dictate the paths our present thoughts take until we overlay them with a new layer of reality just like new asphalt on an Interstate Highway.

Results from new scientific research generate hope. Scientists are loading new awareness on a little train and sending it off on its way to people who are hurting. But, awareness is not enough. Once the train pulls into a victim's station, the victim is charged with two steps: decision and action. A decision must be made to enlist generals to lead the campaign, and action must be taken to find the right generals. Wars are not fought in one theater of operation but on many different battlefields. The importance of each must be prioritized.

An over-all strategy must be planned, one based on intelligence gathered from all available sources. It is vital that each person's strategy be custom designed because brains are not all alike. There are: healthy brains, emotionally damaged brains, brains damaged from disease, brains damaged from injuries, or brains misformed from birth.

As in any war, plans must be designed to fit the terrain. If an army is sent to a desert campaign outfitted with down jackets, wool mittens and foot heaters in heavy boots, it probably will not be victorious.

Over a hundred years ago, Pierre Janet wrote about the breakdown of adaptation in psychological trauma. He wrote about a breakdown in the body's normal ability to receive new information, find the pigeonhole it fits into in the brain's existing stored information, and adapt and respond to the new integrated body of information. In 1889, he published a book *L'automatisme Psychologique* about his investigations into the mental processes that transform traumatic experiences into mental illnesses. The first to systematically study dissociation as the crucial process in reaction to overwhelming experiences, he showed that traumatic memories may later surface as sensory perceptions, emotions, or by the victim reenacting the event.

In the book he points out that even before his writings scientists drew attention to the way in which certain happenings would leave indelible and distressing memories. He points out that sufferers continually returned to these memories and were tormented by them day and night. Janet's ideas of an integrated approach were widely accepted and respected during his day but soon faded as scientists developed their studies along divergent paths in their own independent fields of study. Interest in the effects of emotions after a trauma was short-lived, and for about sixty years after about 1890 only a few studies were done. The studies that have been done since dealt mainly with emotions after wars and the Holocaust.

Now, the battle cry is being sounded again to look at the problem with a broader view. The battle cry has become FIND THE BALANCE between mind, body and soul. There are three points to our lives: mind, body and soul. When one gets out of balance, like a boot on a tire, our lives don't run smoothly.

The use of external chemicals alone is rarely sufficient to heal Post Traumatic Stress Disorder. However, because it relieves the pain of symptoms, it helps a patient to better participate in, and therefore get more benefit from, programs to identify and overcome the cause. There are people who argue against the use of medication on the basis that it only deals with the symptoms, not the underlying disease causing the symptoms. They argue that if the symptoms leave, the patients will leave also. Yes, they might. However, it seems reasonable that any disorder that can last for decades if left untreated involves physical changes and, at least for some period, calls for physical intervention.

Among the work of other researchers, the work done at the National Center for Post Traumatic Stress Disorder in West Haven, Connecticut, explains ways changes occur in the brain. Changes occur in the locus ceruleus (which regulates the brain's secretion of hormones that mobilize the body for an emergency); in the increase in secretion of CRF, (a hormone that mobilizes the body to meet an emergency); and in the opiate system of the brain (which can blunt the feeling of pain). This work shows irregularities in these brain systems.

Dr. Wayne H. Peterson of Phoenixville, Pennsylvania, warns that dissociation and some seizure episodes have similar symptoms. Unless seizures are ruled out first, cases may be misdiagnosed. These two problems are often confused but their brain processes, and therefore required treatments, are markedly different. As a result, people can be hurt by long treatment programs that eventually fail or by being repeatedly admitted to one mental health care institution after another. People with minimal brain damage are also at high risk for having the true cause of their pain overlooked. If the symptoms are ones that can be caused by many different things, (and other things are more obvious), minimal brain damage may not command the attention needed to be heeded.

It is imperative that the Commanding General chosen to be in charge of the campaign to overthrow the Inner Silent Dictator be one who believes in, and insists on, an interdisciplinary strategy using the expertise and cooperation of a whole staff of capable generals. It is also imperative that it be one who is capable and willing to look past just one battlefield. Just because some events that cause post traumatic stress are not as dramatic or as easily identified as others does not mean the victim's pain is any less. The battle must be fought in all theaters of operation where it exists, not just the obvious ones.

Chapter XVII

WHERE DO YOU FIND A HERO?

Heroes are needed in any conflict of a just cause. Wars expose heroes; they do not create them. Heroes are everywhere among us, waiting for their draft call. As with any potential conscripts, some get a call, some are never called. The day the devastating fireball careened across an Iowa cornfield like a giant projectile of lightening, many heroes got their call.

What is a hero? The role of hero doesn't come upon a person suddenly. It's the way a person lives, day in and day out. Sometimes, in a time of crisis, the role is more publicly apparent, but most of the time the behavior isn't new. Usually, a person continues to respond in a new situation the same way his or her brain has been taught to respond. In the case of a crisis, it is the situation that is different, not the person. There is little time to plan. The brain goes on automatic pilot. As a rule, a crisis is a time of re-action, not a time of action.

It isn't always easy being a hero. Captain Haynes spoke about the role of hero that he and his fellow crew members now live with. While in Sioux City two and a half years after the crash during the premier showing of the TV movie *Crash Landing: The Rescue Of Flight 232*, he talked to reporters.

CAPT. HAYNES: You just accept it. It happened and there's nothing you can do about it.

Capt. Haynes is known to have had a hard time with the idea when (as he calls it) "the hero thing" started to build. His feeling was that it was nonsense, that he and the crew were just doing their jobs. A company psychiatrist's position was that it was none of Haynes' business.

CAPTAIN HAYNES: What do you mean it's none of my business? They're talking about us.

PSYCHIATRIST: People have heroes for themselves. They don't have heroes for the heroes. If they need to have heroes right now, they need it, and it happens to be you and the crew. The best thing you crew can do is just accept it for the people's benefit.

That was a lot to think about for a man as modest and unassuming as Capt. Haynes. There was a lot for the whole community to think about after the crash. People tend to try to avoid and deny thoughts of things that are horrible because to think that something like that could happen scares us. So, to shield us from such pain, our mind puts an umbrella of a that-only-happens-to-the-other-guy coating over such ideas. This only protects us temporarily, however, because bad things do happen in good lives. Life does not always run smoothly. There are patches of sunshine and patches of rain.

The community as a whole, and also as individuals, went through a severe period of secondary trauma. The devastation of the tragedy was just as thorough as the devastation of some of the battles in Vietnam. The emotions generated were similar. The secondary trauma, too, was similar to what the families left at home when loved ones left to fight the war in Vietnam went through. In many cases, it was also as unrecognized.

The reporting of the crash of Flight 232 was brought into the living rooms of people all over the world. In the same manner, the vivid reporting of the Vietnam war graphically brought the high level of trauma Tim was going through right into his family's living room. (Family names have been changed.) His wife Shirley had to personally battle the effects of the secondary trauma as well as battle the effects of it on her three young sons. In addition, she had to take responsibility in many areas that she and her husband had shared until that time and also in many areas that were considered "men's work" by traditional values of that era. Today this role switch is much more accepted, but it was a radical departure from accepted thinking in the 1960's.

Suddenly Shirley and her children, and others like them, had to deal with the combination of stresses of:

- loneliness from loss of companionship,
- support of their mates,
- the uprooting of their whole families from familiar home environments they had established,
- changing accepted roles of behavior,
- assuming the total responsibility for raising their children,
- and of total lack of understanding of what they were going through from many civilian friends and neighbors in their new neighborhoods.

In addition to her own pain, as a mother Shirley absorbed the reflected pain of her children's losses. Many people tend to think (probably because of young children's immature language skills) that they do not understand what is going on around them and are not affected by the intensity of feelings that adults are. Children do feel intense feelings and, if stress is not released, also store them in their bodies.

Shirley was pregnant when her husband received his orders for Vietnam. Shirley had the baby (couldn't stop that); they finished the house (decided not to stop that); and moved into a home she was now only going to live in a few months. Baby Harry was six months old when his father left for a year in Vietnam. He lived his first year and a half in an atmosphere of fear and anxiety. Shirley was *physically* there and planned exciting activities for the family to pass the year but she was not *emotionally* there for them. Her primary emotion that year was agonizing fear of the future; all other emotions were secondary. Harry still suffers from free floating anxiety and depression. Emotions have dissociated from events in the past, so separating the effects of emotions generated in the present and emotions generated in the past is difficult.

Dick, two-and-a-half-years-old, was saddened by his father's leaving. All the family went to the airport to see Tim off - Dick, his two brothers, his mother and grandparents from both sides. After a full keep-a-stiff-upper-lip routine of hugs and kisses, his father boarded the plane and it took off. Everybody waved until "Daddy's plane" was out of sight, then Shirley assured them "Daddy said he's coming right back." In the months that followed, every time a plane passed over the boys would yell "Daddy's plane, Daddy's plane." One day Shirley saw Dick, almost three years old by then, sitting on his tricycle staring at a plane high in the sky during the whole length of the time it was within view. Then he rode it up to her and, with a pained look on is face, said "Sure Daddy comin' right back?" Of course, Shirley wasn't sure he was coming back, not sure at all. Dick's life is still beset with fear of abandonment issues. He tends to re-enact his past abandonment in the present by choosing behaviors and relationships in the present that set him up for abandonment. Choices and behaviors have predictable consequences. However obviously predictable they may be to other people, they may be temporarily hidden from a person suffering from post traumatic stress. Our brain just works that way.

For some people, the healing grief process takes a long time. We, in America, are used to the McDonald's Fast Food Mentality. We have learned to expect to get food fast and we expect to have pain end fast, but it doesn't work that way. Releasing the neuromessengers that transmit the message of pain takes time. There is no time table for grief. Grief lasts until its work is done. Some people get stuck temporarily on the step of awareness and confusion. Some people never go further than this step. Their decision to remain dependent personalities—dependent on other people, places or things to spoon feed them their attitudes and fill their needs—is a decision by default.

Tom was eight years old at the time his father left. He was probably the child affected most. Being older, he had more time to build a bonded friendship with his father. He also had the monkey of responsibility put on his back by a remark routinely made to the oldest son of the family by military men of that era as they were leaving for an extended absence. "You're the father while I'm gone. Take care of Mom." Meant as a role of honor, in hindsight military families learned that it was too much responsibility to assign to young boys. Young children take their parents' spoken or unspoken assignments very seriously. Young servomechanisms fight very hard to carry out instructions given them even though a young child's stage of development and abilities are totally incapable of doing so, or of even understanding what it is they are supposed to do. However, based on the limited understanding at that time of how the brain worked, no one could have even suspected the inner conflict set in motion.

There was another current churning inside of Tom—a fantasy, severed from reality, bringing visual images before his mind that Shirley didn't know about until later in the year. In his mind, Tom had picked out the date that his father was going to be killed in Vietnam. Before Tim left, the family had lived in a community where many of the fathers were helicopter pilots and rotated back and forth to Vietnam yearly. Tom and his close friend, whose father was in Vietnam when they lived there, were eagerly awaiting his return. They marked the days off on the friend's calendar. Three weeks before he was to come home, Tom's friend's father was killed. Tom's mind had concluded, in a way children's minds sometimes think, that his father, too, would be killed three weeks before his date to come home. He didn't tell Shirley. He was, after all, charged with the responsibility of protecting Mom as surrogate father. He fought his inner battle in silence; he suffered alone.

As the date approached, Tom had little energy left for second grade schoolwork. He spent most of his time staring out the window, attending to the war and his father's danger. The teacher in the civilian community they had moved into for the year to be near the grandparents while Tim was in Vietnam, knew or cared little about the problems of military families. Totally unsympathetic, she treated it as a discipline problem. This was child abuse of the highest order but, at that time, parents were trained not to question teachers' judgment because society vested them with complete authority.

As the date in Tom's mind approached, he could not stay in a dark bedroom because he saw the images of war. He still had not spoken out. As the date grew even nearer, he could not sleep. He finally told Shirley that when he closed his eyes he saw men fighting the war on the inside of his eyelids. At this point she made an appointment for him with a military psychologist. But after the appointment when Shirley told the teacher the findings of the doctor, trying to enlist her help, the teacher's only remark was "I doubt that." There was never any understanding or cooperation. Tim continued to get severe punishments and detentions for staring out the window.

It was a very hard year for Tom but, when his father came home, the family moved on and put the emotions of the year behind them as society of that era required. The losses of that year have never been grieved and, as he was taught as a child to do, Tom still lives his life suppressing emotions.

Shirley and her sons, now grown men, still live with the aftermath of living for a year in fear and anxiety. The subconscious habits that her sons were taught as children are now inhibiting their chances for happy lives as adults. Because they deliberately suppressed their emotions when Tim came home from Vietnam so they could get on with their lives, chemical molecules were buried. They remain buried and, when triggered by an event in the present, still stimulate and influence feelings and reactions in the present.

Emotions that are blocked and buried at the time of a trauma rise to the surface after people get back to a normal lifestyle and have time to realize what they did, or didn't, do. Feelings of anxiety, anger and guilt result. Memories might bubble up in the form of sudden, unexplainable sadness or tears.

The losses generated by the secondary trauma in friends and family of the primary victim must be grieved. This, to a great extent, has been ignored until this era of breaking the silence. There is an element of survivor guilt in this pattern of looking away, this pattern of avoidance. The military man's losses in having to go to war are so great that, by comparison, losses of families left at home seem insignificant. They aren't. The losses are real and, as with any other loss, the pain remains until it is grieved.

Relatives and loved ones left at home tend to focus on the danger of the fighting man. Little energy is left to pay attention to the cancerous feelings gnawing inside. In most cases, in order to survive these feelings must be suppressed during the time of the separation. When the fighting man returns, the tendency is to try to dissociate from the past pain. This leaves the pain still locked inside the body, still acting on the subconscious level. Our bodies are designed to constantly seek harmony. So, if we block this pain from moving through our bodies and being released in the natural way, it will find alternate, less healthy, ways to express the stress. Today we know that there is a long list of stress illnesses the body can choose from.

Men returning from a war zone expect, and have a right to expect, a happy reunion. Often it isn't. Men rotating from duty in Vietnam, as well as men returning from the Gulf War, found that not only had their lives changed but so had the lives of their families. After having been told they were fighting a war to preserve their way of life, many found that their very absence had changed it. This caught some by surprise because many people didn't understand the secondary trauma experienced by people who love and depend upon those involved in a primary trauma.

Because of pain still inside Vietnam vets, new information is being discovered about how the brain and mind work. As more is understood today about the pain still inside friends and relatives of Vietnam vets (and also the connection between it and problems in their present lives) more is being understood about the pain still inside Emergency First Responders and friends and relatives of all types of catastrophic events as well.

People who choose the field of Emergency Response are people who care about the needs of others. Research being done by Ronald C. Kessler and Jane D. McLeod of the Institute for Social Research, Ann Arbor, Michigan, is indicating that there is an emotional cost to caring, and that there are differences in men's and women's vulnerability to undesirable life events. In the past, most people have thought that this was because women's traditional roles are more stressful and less fulfilling than men's traditional roles. Kessler and McLeod, on the other hand, studied differences in exposure and response to trauma. Their work showed that although men and women have about the same number of undesirable events, women are more emotionally affected than men. Men and women are taught to play different roles in life. According to author Carol Gilligan, women are taught a moral sense that emphasizes nurturing and caring for others; men are taught a moral sense that emphasizes individual rights and responsibilities. Except for traumas that affect their spouses and children, women are more affected by events that occur to people that are important to them than men are.

Women are taught that their role of nurturing extends beyond the circle of their spouse and children. Because of this, they are more exposed to secondary trauma. More events occur in their networks than to their individual family members. Although most men know more people than women do, women are more aware when people around them are troubled. In many instances, people are used to looking to the women rather than the men around them for support and comfort in times of trouble.

The survey shows that women have more friends with life crises than men and that women are more emotionally affected by them when they happen. There might be two possibilities for this greater reporting of exposure by women. They might actually know of more network crises than men; and they might define a wider range of people as significant others than men.

Emergency First Responders such as EMTs, firemen, security personnel, etc., who assist at the scene of crises are affected by this secondary trauma. Psychological counselors and members of the clergy who work with relatives and close friends are particularly vulnerable.

People are all different, and each comes into a crisis with a different schema (systematic arrangement in their brains of all their previous thoughts and experiences). Because new sounds, smells and images must fit into this existing schema and be filtered through it, each person's reaction to a particular crisis is different.

Three years have passed now since the crash of United Flight 232 and, in interviewing three men who were first responders and who now play key roles in crisis management, variations in responses are obvious.

Jeff Peterson is now Director of Disaster Services for the American Red Cross in Sioux City but was managing one of the city's public swimming pools at the time of the crash.

JEFF: I was on the site at the airport as a volunteer working in the morgue. I remember very little. It seems that at the time I saw very little. Because the scenes were so horrible, I think I developed tunnel vision and only saw what was directly related to the job I was assigned to do. I remember the names of two particular women because these were the people I was told to report to. I now work with these women on projects in connection with my job as Red Cross Disaster Services Director. They played very important, and very visible, roles in the coordination of the work at the morgue.

I don't remember seeing them there.

On November 12, 1991, the American Red Cross signed an agreement with the American Psychological Association to develop a plan for psychological services to be used at the time of a disaster. Jeff emphasizes that it is important that this plan be designed not only for victims, friends and family, but also for trained workers sent to the site. As a professional, he is sent on such assignments. He talked about his on-site work during the crisis of Hurricane Hugo in 1989.

JEFF: I worked in Vega Baja, about 35 miles straight west from San Juan, Puerto Rico. When sent on assignments like that, a worker is required to agree to a minimum of three weeks—three weeks in a lonely hotel room—three weeks under tremendous stress—three weeks away from family, friends and established support people—at a time when their personal support is most needed.

He talked about the victims . . . about people who have sometimes lost family members and everything else except the clothes on their backs. Often, all the relationships and material possessions that made up their lifestyle have suddenly been snatched away from them. At that moment, the only tie they feel they have left is this American Red Cross worker. Often, there are thousands of them at a time. It is very draining on the worker.

Yes, Jeff can testify that there is a need for a plan for services. . .a plan to cover both the time of the disaster and the time after. A plan for aftercare is essential, both for the victims and for professionals.

The disaster plan used in Sioux City during the response to United Flight 232 included psychological services, but the sheer numbers of people who needed the services overwhelmed the plan. At the time of the disaster it was expanded to include two site coordinators, one based at the airport and one based at the location where friends and relatives were being cared for.

The community's disaster preparedness plan mental health services representative, Don McCulley, Director of Siouxland Mental Health, was the site coordinator at the airport. Groups that worked at the airport dealt mainly with emergency responders and volunteers directly involved with putting out the burning airplane, locating survivors and getting them to the city's two hospitals, with identifying bodies, and dealing with the physical wreckage of the plane. One hospital is a major Trauma Center and the other a Regional Burn Center, so many of the responders were highly trained and experienced professionals. Because of experience in disasters, they understood the importance of on-site debriefing as a tool to help emergency personnel cope with the combination of stresses they were experiencing.

Emergency workers such as ambulance, police, fire, sheriff, rescue and hospital personnel are personally affected by the stress of the work they do. Critical incident stress debriefing (CISD) on the site can help keep the flow of emotions moving through the body.

The visual images being imprinted on the brain, the mixture of smells intermingling and overpowering the senses, the long hours of tension and toil all took their toll. Although past experience and training helped in many ways, certain types of past experiences placed added stress on some. Workers who had been in air crashes themselves, people who were currently grieving the death of a loved one, veterans of similar death and destruction in Vietnam all had to cope with double doses of stress.

Debriefing sessions were held at the site during the time of the crisis. Then free, open to the public debriefing sessions were scheduled in convenient locations for weeks after the crash. There came a time when Don decided the job was done. In television and newspaper interviews, he said he would no longer talk about it. He told people the crisis was over and it was time for the community to put it behind and get on with its life. Some community leaders followed suit.

A Survivors and Family Services Center was established to house and care for the needs of surviving passengers and families of surviving and non-surviving passengers. Mental health professionals from four states, representing every facility within 60 miles, arrived at the center to offer their services. There were more volunteers than could even be used.

Dr. Gerald Jacobs, Department of Psychology, University of South Dakota, assumed responsibility of site coordinator at this location. During the four and a half days after the crash a large number of ministers, priests, nuns, rabbis, and members of the Church of Jesus Christ of Latter-Day Saints ministered and provided support to survivors and families. A University of South Dakota team of sixteen clinical graduate students provided more then 600 hours of mental health services. Students in the university's doctoral program in clinical psychology receive 20 hours of hot-line training, including crisis intervention, in the first semester. The people working at this location agreed, as their assignment, to (a) care for the survivors by providing access to qualified mental health professions and (b) to protect them from overeager reporters, attorneys, and sightseers.

Day shifts for volunteers at the Survivors and Family Services Center were eleven hours long, with eight-hour evening and night shifts. Shifts for the site coordinators at both locations were longer.

The counselors did far more than traditional therapy. They assisted families get information requested by the airlines, medical examiner or funeral directors. They helped arriving families find out if their loved ones were alive or dead and, when needed, got the proper attention for family members when a death notice arrived. They went with family members to claim personal effects and helped make funeral arrangements when necessary. They assisted those with physical emergencies or handicaps.

In this new era of breaking the silence, our society is beginning to see that the pain of the secondary trauma does not stop when the last media person leaves a crash site. Nor did it stop when the veterans came home. Shirley can see that the pain of her secondary trauma did not stop when her husband came home from Vietnam; nor did his.

It wasn't over when it was over.

It was almost twenty years later before the focus of research began to connect the problems many Vietnam vets and their families were having in their present lives with the trauma the men had experienced during their tours of duty. The men and their families unknowingly lived silently with it all that time. After his return, Tim's and Shirley's relationship, which had been spontaneous and open before he was sent to Vietnam, had an area separated from her by a wall of avoidance and denial. For him, things had to run through a filter of protection. Through the next twenty years, as their family ran into rough spots—as all families do—this area of emotional separateness widened.

Crises were never resolved; painful events were avoided and denied. Issues that caused problems were never talked about because, under the pattern that had by then been established of "let's put problems behind us and get on with our lives", the law of silence ruled. There was no pressure release valve. The traditional way of thinking at that time was to forget the past and move forward. Because they could not face, or even identify, the issues causing the problems, the pressure built. One day, because there was no safety valve, the pressure cooker blew up. Because the habit of avoidance and denial was so firmly established, during a time of severe family crisis, Tim left. Now, because of new research that shows how the brain actually works, rather than the way scientists thought for long that it worked, Shirley knows this is typical and can now better understand that their relationship followed a predictable pattern. At the time she didn't, nor did he.

That was years ago. She's older now, but many of the physical chemicals stored at the time are still trapped in her body. New medical research now shows that our bodies don't forget the past, they just put it in storage.

Chapter XVIII

WILL THE LAST THIRD OF OUR LIVES BE A PERIOD OF LIBERATION OR SIEGE?

On another night when I was at the condo, Carolyn, the sensitive and exciting lady I met at the public speaking seminar, came out and we grilled steaks on the balcony. Since Liz missed her steak and I had bought an extra one for each time I had invited guests, I wound up eating Teriyaki steaks five nights out of the seven I was in that condo. I haven't eaten one since. Among other things, Carolyn and I talked about the effect stored emotions can have as people get older.

Just as certain environments are more stressful than others, certain ages are more stressful than others. The stresses generated in the last third of our lives by growing older, or by having someone we love grow older, are different than the stresses of the first and second thirds. Because they are different, we need to plan for them differently. There is stress in the first third of our lives as it is spent in learning the things needed to become independent. As children, we are dependent on the adults around us to fill our needs while we learn the skills to fit into our society and be productive enough to fill our own needs. In the second third of our lives, we must adapt to the stresses of being productive in the workplace and guiding our children, if we have any, in the paths that experience has taught us will help them most. Also, we must adjust to the fear and confusion of mid-life, admit and accept our own mortality.

In the last third of our lives, we reap the harvest of the seeds we've sown. For some, it is best to delay picking it until we get a few of the weeds out and add new fertilizer-thoughts to nourish the plants that are yielding positive produce. Our self-honesty, openness to allow new awareness to take root and willingness to make changes based on the ideas and opportunities triggered by these new awareness comes into play.

Elderly people who have not released chemicals stored during traumatic events or periods in their lives are at high risk for post traumatic stress. Having denied and avoided experiencing the pain for years, even decades, they come to the point where there is little time left for procrastination. This realization is often expressed in feelings of depression and reassignment to too little time. As inner conflict grows, the downward spiral of depression starts and inertia gets a foothold. Listless days are spent in an armchair or rocker, a bowed head occasionally supported by a hand on the forehead. As memories of the past come, so does the silence. Symptoms of depression such as loss of interest in appearance, keeping house or eating, begin to appear. The siege of unrecognized emotions generating from unresolved issues—sometimes stored after events as far back as childhood—must be annihilated at this time before some senior citizens can be liberated to enjoy this period.

Sometimes misconceptions and distorted thinking must be corrected. Because of taboos placed by society in the past about talking about many of the problems that cause trauma and pain, misconceptions and distorted thinking resulting from childhood events are common. This silence can now be broken. The pain can be released. Although at this age many of the people involved are dead, psychological tools like the Family Reconstruction tool are helpful by providing an opportunity for a senior citizen to go back in time and take a look at past events with maturity rather than the child when the events happened.

We are what we think. Our perceptions, whether myth or reality, determine our decisions and our actions. A funny thing is happening right now. The "youth culture" which has been used to so much attention is getting older. With the tremendous strides in the medical field, it's members are still feeling alert and active. Now, viewing the situation from this new vantage point, they see no reason to pass the mantle, or the attention, to those with less experience.

In doing geriatric research to write this chapter, my excitement grew as my awareness of the implications of current geriatric research grew. Discoveries are opening up wonderful possibilities for the last third of people's lives. Robert Terry, professor of Neurosciences and Pathology at the University of California at San Diego found that many neurons don't actually die but simply shrink. Anders Bjorklund, of Lund University in Sweden, has been successful in improving elderly rats' memories by injecting them with nerve growth factors. My excitement lead me to throw my energies into the ElderHelp Peer Counseling Program. What better person to help a senior citizen work through the emotions after a trauma, and to help custom design a new lifestyle, than someone who is already using, and feeling the benefits of, available programs and services?

When designed and run in cooperation with consultants knowledgeable of and responsive to the new findings in geriatrics, ElderHelp Peer Counseling Programs can be of great help. They can help senior citizens deal with their current issues and emotional problems and help them understand their behavior and how it affects others around them. They can provide an opportunity for mutual support and can be a help in adjusting to the stresses of adapting to declining abilities and resources. ElderHelp groups can provide an opportunity to make new friendships at a time when there has been a loss of old friends by death or relocation. The opportunity to be of help to one another gives a new feeling of worth and increases self-esteem. The groups common goals can provide a format for senior citizens to remain stimulated, active and connected to others.

ElderHelp Peer Counseling Programs can also help correct the distorted thinking in the last third of our lives that we are too old for sports, sex, learning new things, acquiring new skills, helping others, or working at new jobs. Senior citizens can help each other learn how to use adaptive defense mechanisms, to find courage to fight the tendency to avoid facing things that frighten, and to attack fears that inhibit and limit life's choices.

Physical illness or injury, sexual difficulties, death of a spouse or other loved one, or choices about retirement and financial readjustment are not problems unique to older people. But, older people are more likely than any other group to have two or more of these problems hitting them at the same time. With increasing age comes increasing frequency of the dreaded phone calls or visits relaying the news that a loved one has died. Whether the death is sudden or one expected for a long time, grief is painful. In a very short period of time, older people may have to overcome the emotions of quite a number of stressful changes. Mutual support provides the opportunity to help each other identify and learn skills to compensate for declining resources. Because new friendships are formed at a time when there is loss of old friends by death, the continuity of the group rather than individual friends helps older people remain stimulated, active and more oriented.

In addition to improving personal relationships, group feedback can help build self-esteem and self-confidence, decrease feelings of helplessness and anger and help make life happier. The goal of ElderHelp is to assist a senior citizen choose options that will result in fewer complaints, help him or her make and keep friends of both sexes, and to have sexual relationships where there is still interest and capacity.

By becoming aware of and being helped to understand and use professionals knowledgeable in specialized areas, older people can better identify and relieve tension generated by either biological or cultural origins. They can learn to work and play within their own personal limits determined by physical condition, past training and activities, the way they view themselves, and what they're interested in.

Some people are hit by a surprise attack as they enter the last third of their lives. People who have unknowingly been using work as a mask to avoid painful emotions suddenly have this defense armor stripped from them. Retirement contains this often unrecognized loss for some people. A successful career, often coupled with workaholism, is a very effective tool when used to avoid having to feel pain. With no tightly filled schedule, no pressure of deadlines, no human support of networking - with only a gold watch methodically ticking away like the nagging of submerged pain tapping to be released, the dam of denial definitely weakens. For many, this is the first time in their lives they have been forced to look inward. Unfortunately, by this time the accumulation of excess baggage, collected like vacation souvenirs along life's way, is often gargantuan. The skills and tools people choose at this point to equip themselves for life's new engagements will determine whether they enter a period of liberation or siege.

There is another piece of intelligence that people over 65 must recognize and factor into the campaign strategy. Our society, with its emphasis on youth and physical beauty, has brainwashed many to think that productive lives are over, or at least diminished in quality, with maturity and its form of beauty.

THAT'S MYTH #1 ABOUT THE
LAST THIRD OF OUR LIVES.

If proper intelligence is gathered and a proper strategy drawn up and implemented, this can be the keenest time in our lives. As "keenagers", we must now ask ourselves the same question we asked as teenagers: "What do I want to be when I grow up?" We are different people now. The many answers that come to mind will also be different.

Relaxing on the balcony, Carolyn and I talked about another lady we had both met for the first time at the public speaking seminar. Author and public speaker Gladys Hotchkiss of Crestline, California is an encourager. She is also a California

Senior Legislator. Perhaps the two are the same. The difference is the first is inborn, the second is an elected position. The California Senior Legislature meets once a year in Sacramento to develop legislation concerning California's four million senior citizens. Voters who elect these legislators must be sixty years of age. Gladys and the other legislators work throughout the year to develop working relationships with state and national legislators and their staffs. Senior Legislators are non-partisan. They represent the best interests of all seniors in California.

Gladys (wife, mother of three daughters, and grandmother of seven) believes, and lives a life that demonstrates, that it is never too late to begin again regardless of one's current situation. She believes that the years beyond sixty can be the best of all years because we can choose to age with passionate pleasure. Traditionally, depression was considered normal in older people. Few doctors took the time to treat it because most felt nothing worked anyway. Three things are changing that attitude:

- growth of the elderly population
- availability of new medications,
- a new understanding of how the brain works.

Contrary to traditional thinking, it is now accepted that psychotherapy can be effective in treating depressed elderly. In most cases, however, the traditional non-directive approach (in which therapists suggest no course of action, give no advice, and rely solely on the patients' insight to figure it out for themselves) is not effective with elderly depressed. Most elderly ask, and need help with, the question "What should I do?"

First, older people must select the terrain and begin the campaign to be victorious over the blahs which defeat some people in maturity. There are general categories of groups older people can consider joining. The first category is people who are still connected to their families. This category is subdivided into those who still live in their own homes and those who can no longer live in their own homes but who are still closely connected to their families.

My elderly Aunt Lorena still lives on the acreage, although not in the same house, which includes land of the family homestead where my Uncle Mid brought her as a bride almost eighty years ago. As soon as funds were available, the young couple built the house in which she still lives. One daughter lives with her; another lives just down the road on property that used to be included in the acreage, but which she and her husband now own. Two other daughters and their families live on acreage's nearby. They are still a close, extended family enjoying the pleasures, and responsibilities, of a three-generation lifestyle. When the parents work or have other commitments, the grandchildren still "visit" their grandmother. Many farm families continue this lifestyle.

Some elderly persons, however, are no longer able to stay in their own homes. Because of physical reasons, they move into group living arrangements but are still closely connected to their families. Unless the emotional aspects of choosing a group home to live in are given adequate time and attention, conflicting emotions can generate pain for years to come. If the conflicting emotions of choosing group care are not identified, and the negative ones adapted to, this choice can often be viewed as a failure. There are several types of group homes.

> **Old-age homes** and **board-and-care** homes are homes where older people are expected to live the rest of their lives. No attempt is made to rehabilitate them for discharge. Instead, they are helped to adjust to a protective setting where they can have a better social life than they could in their own homes.
>
> **Nursing homes** and **extended-care facilities** are for long-term care of chronically ill or impaired people. They emphasize admission of short-term convalescent patients with potential for rehabilitation to community life.
>
> **Day-care centers** and **community centers for the aged** provide places for older persons to

meet, socialize, and work though feelings of anxiety, boredom, depression, and loneliness.

A new trend is **retirement communities of relatively healthy older people** who live and work together. These communities may have an associated medical facility and may be designed around a common interest, such as golf.

Older people with no connection to friends or family make up another category. Some of these people spend their days in isolation, either by choice or as a result of financial restrictions. Perhaps they have outlived all of their friends and family. Perhaps they are women who were forced by their society's views in their day to make a decision between a career and a family. When I graduated from college, all my job interviews contained questions about who I was dating, for how long, and about my intentions of marriage. My answers were then analyzed as to my suitability for the job opening. In my day, women were terminated from many jobs when they married. It was simply the accepted tradition in the restrictive Southern culture, tradition backed up by state laws in some cases.

Some older people have no family but are connected to an extended family through a loving organization such as a church or hospital sponsored program. Meals-On-Wheels, or Home Health and Housekeeping programs are examples.

In their book *We've Got To Do Something About Mother*, Dr. J. Ryan and Marilyn Richardson of South Dakota State University discuss the problem of trying to find the right care for older people. This decision affects not only frail or disabled elderly people, but also people who take on the role of their caretakers. Many of these caretakers are over sixty-five themselves. Emotions of joy and satisfaction, as well as anger, resentment, jealousy, guilt and remorse surface in both the caretaker and the one being cared for.

The book was written as a result of the stress they experienced in caring for Mother in their own home. They found several excellent books that gave factual information on many aspects of caring for aging adults, but few addressed the emotional demands. Realizing that caretakers in similar situations need support material, they interviewed people with unique problems or point of view: family infighting, a male nurse stealing $20,000 from the family, a woman lost in the Denver airport. The stories of the people they interviewed made them realize that there is a need for reassurance that feelings experienced are within the normal range, and that the caretaker is not alone. Marilyn states that she hopes the openness and honesty of these stories can serve to trigger discussions between people who need to talk about what should be done and how to proceed.

My friend Carol found herself facing this problem. I asked her if she would be willing to try to express her feelings on paper for inclusion in this book. The article she sent me in return, which I am including in its entirety prefaced by her cover letter, touched me deeply because my mother, too, spent her last years in a group home run by a caring staff. For my mother, too, it was a period of making new friends and of enjoyable experiences with her own 90-years-plus peer group.

CAROL'S LETTER: I've thought and thought and thought about what to write for you, and have simply decided to send you this article I wrote and let you pick and choose. Perhaps the saddest of all feelings was my inability to make life more comfortable for my mother. No matter what I did, I couldn't "make her better." I lived in a state of sadness for five years. Yet, a nursing home was the only choice. Mother needed help I couldn't provide. Although her being there gave me peace of mind for I knew she had 24-hour care, I felt bad because it wasn't her home, although it *was* her home. Feelings of helplessness filled my being because I couldn't provide all her needs. In my eyes, I failed.

The staff was marvelous, for the most part. Yet, when a loved one is in a care home, someone must be there to *listen* to that person, no matter how frustrating or inconsequential their complaints are. I knew always that I had to "be there" for her.

And yet there were so many times when I couldn't be there. I struggled minute by minute with feelings of anger, guilt, aloneness, and grief—as did she.

I also felt torn—between filling the needs of my husband, the needs of my mother, and my own needs. And I wondered what I was supposed to do, and who was I that anybody should need me. I cried myself to sleep—more than once—because I wasn't caring for her. And I prayed to God each night to let me be with her when she left. And He did. What more could I ask?

Emily, my special friend, these are my feelings—probably not all of them but the ones that lie close to the surface. Use all, part, or none, or make me do a better job.

WHAT A DIFFERENCE A DAY MAKES

From Home To Nursing Home

by Carol O'Hara

"I'll *never* put my Mother in a nursing home," I cried, racing through the back door to the garage on a rain drenched January night. My dash was in answer to a call from a nurse in the emergency room at one of our major hospitals.

"Your mother's had an accident. It's her left hip," she said, "but drive slowly and carefully. She's all right."

Drive slowly? How could I? Mother was 88. She'd already had hip replacement surgery on her right hip. Now her left hip. The nurse's words couldn't be true. But they were. And Mother's life changed. She never walked again.

Oh, her life had changed before, but never quite so drastically. Twenty years or so ago I'd helped her move from the home she'd shared with my Dad until his death. Together we'd sorted, saved, given away, and tossed away a lifetime of treasures and trash. We'd agonized over which pieces of furniture to keep and which pieces to sell. We'd struggled with the safe packing of china tea cups and crystal goblets. We'd cried when we'd come across old photographs. And we'd laughed over some as well.

But eventually, Mother and I made the decisions, and a new life for her with her favorite things awaited in a lovely retirement apartment set amidst roses, winding walks, and bridges over manmade creeks. We had selected this particular site with great care. Mother was happy. She was free of the heavy yard care and the worry of a roof that could leak at any minute. She made new friends, hung the Christmas tree lights on her patio, and cooked wonderful meals for my family and for them.

Then illness forced her to a new level of living wherein she had help. Instead of her doing necessary chores, and the cooking, a staff did the work and prepared food for her and for others like her, leaving Mother free to simply enjoy herself. She no longer drove, but she wanted to stay as independent as she could. So, with help, she took cabs to her favorite shopping mall and to her hairdresser, and she rode the marvelous Paratransit to doctor appointments. Like she had done before, she made herself content, and I no longer worried about her being alone.

But her move from her apartment to what the professionals call residential care was, as it is for most adult children of aging parents, difficult for me. This time, I had to make the initial search for her new home without her.

I visited each retirement village that offered residential (or as it is often called, intermediate) care. I spoke with the staff and with those who lived there. I inspected the entire premises of every one. I also made certain I ate at least one meal at each home, and I looked to see if the silver and dishes were really clean. I watched the way the personnel conducted themselves. I ranked the top ones in my thinking and took Mother to visit each. She needed to have the ultimate decision.

She now was moving from an apartment with a bedroom to a studio apartment. Again, her furniture and household possessions had to be sorted. But the decisions were too difficult for her to make. This time, it was up to me. Where would her china cabinet go? To sale, to storage, or into my home? What would I do with the great big mahogany Magnavox radio-phonograph-television set Dad had won many years ago. Should it stay in the family? Was it junk? How about the everyday silver and the pots and pans? These were not *my* things. They were *Mother's*. What right did I have to make choices about objects that were not mine? I asked myself this question more than once.

No longer was I simply my mother's daughter. I was now, for all practical purposes, the caretaker of her life. And, while I was surrounded by loving family and friends, I felt completely alone. And yes, even abandoned by my frail mother. "How did she become so old so quickly?" I wondered.

But emotion had to be set aside. Her future was at stake. I had to make astute financial decisions, as well as decisions that involved her day-to-day living. Each had to be undertaken with clear thought. So I did what a friend suggested. I detached emotion from my work. It made my task easier. Mother appreciated my care and concern which was gratifying.

She understood that life was indeed changing again. She accepted it, but she had difficulty accepting her failing body. I felt a great need to protect her from her worst enemies—aging and infirmity. I assured her that her home would be kept as intact as possible. I wanted her to know that she could again set up housekeeping, should her health return.

Always Mother had said, "I don't feel I should live with you," and that decision seemed right—until that rainy January night. All I wanted to do then was bring her home with me and "make her better" as she had "made me better" when, as a child, I'd been hurt. However, major surgery to repair her hip and long weeks in the hospital weakened her. I knew I could not give her the professional care she needed. So a new search began. I had to find a full-care home. And I had definite criteria.

It had to be bright. Clean. Cheerful. No bugs or spiders. Mother had to be in an area where the residents were mentally alert for her mind challenged mine. The staff had to be neat. It had to have an excellent physical therapy department. I wanted one close to my home so I could visit often.

My search took me throughout the area where I live. Again, I interviewed staff and residents, tried the food, and surveyed the full environment. But this time I did something else: I used my sense of smell. If unpleasant odors were prevalent, I left.

Only one home met *all* my standards, but there were no rooms at this Inn. I persevered. I won. I collapsed with relief. And another life—for Mother and for me—began. Now, Mother had simply one-half of a room. A curtain divided her from a total stranger. But a caring staff helped her make the transition. And I, becoming more accustomed to sorting, saving, and discarding, did it again—for Mother. This time, she didn't ask "What did you do with my silver?" She knew I'd keep everything she loved—just in case she could have her own apartment again. Most of her home moved into my garage—in boxes.

Together, Mother and I learned that nursing homes are not simply "orphanages for old people." We found out that those residing in nursing homes are not simply folks "left there to die." Nursing homes are small worlds within our great world. The people are real people with wonderful pasts who love to tell their stories to anyone who will take the time to listen. I listened and I was taught.

We learned, too, that there are people of all ages in and out each day—just as there are in any neighborhood. Young children find surrogate grandparents. School children come to tap dance. Volunteers—young and old—come simply to visit or take someone by the hand for a walk. And staff, most of them excellent, come in all ages and in all nationalities.

Mother enjoyed good days and she suffered bad days. But always she had love and care, and the physical help she so desperately needed. And she knew that I was only a phone call away. For I had discovered that adult children of dependent parents are, for the most part, their complete security.

Part Two—THE ESCAPE

Chapter XIX

KNOW THE ENEMY: CHEMICAL IMBALANCE

In order to fight any war, it is necessary to understand the enemy. In order to fight the War Against Silence, we need to become aware of what's going on inside of us. Chemicals are produced in our bodies in response to our associations between ideas. If our minds make distorted associations, it can cause a chemical imbalance. A chemical imbalance can be caused by a conflict between stored information and current information. Chemicals control our moods, productivity and behaviors without our being aware of it on the conscious level.

Neuromessengers were already playing an important part in my life before the crash happened although I didn't understand their role or effects. A question I had not asked myself at the time it happened was "When a marriage of thirty years dissolves after what you both thought was a fun, emotionally close, touch-freely one (given the usual ups and downs of any relationship), are you then an endorphin orphan?" I didn't know anything about endorphins or enkephlines or even what a neuromessenger was. Most lay people don't know anything about chemicals the brain produces, or even that there is a biological basis for behavior. I asked a friend of mine if he knew. "Oh yes, that's that runner's high thing, isn't it?" Yes, it is, but our body's balance of chemicals, and what can happen when they get out of balance, is a lot more than that.

My awareness came quite by accident at a place called Iowa Lakeside Lab as an outgrowth of my interest in environmental issues. I first went to Lakeside Lab, a biology field station on the shores of Lake Okoboji, as part of a volunteer group clearing brush in a prairie management project. The Iowa Lakeside Lab experience is more than what is learned in classes, field trips, or doctoral and post-doctoral research. The topics of researchers who come from all over the world are varied. An important part of the experience is exchange of information in the small groups that gather in cabins, on docks or on verandahs overlooking the lake after dusk brings the day's outdoor research to a halt. The conversations, with their explosions of what-ifs, yes-but-on-the-other-hands, etc., mesh the ideas of a diverse cross-section of scientists.

There, I found out that many studies done with humans begin with work done with animals and water creatures in places such as Lakeside. Dr. Robert Cruden, Acting Director, was excited by the work of students and researchers who come to Lakeside Lab in the summer from all parts of the world. Dr. Mike Lannoo, who teaches at Ball State University during the winter, and his former grad assistant (now Mrs. Sue Lannoo) were doing work with electric fish. The brains of these fish, though far less complex than ours, function the same way as human brains do. Information learned studying them is then transferable to serve as a basis for studies of the human brain.

Although Experiential Education is now becoming widely appreciated, and more and more classes are being taught based on the method, Lakeside Lab has been teaching that way for 90 years. It was founded in 1909 by Thomas McBride on that very concept. Just as Lakeside uses over 130 acres of natural area on the shore of Lake Okoboji for its laboratory method of instruction, Experiential Education uses personal experiences as its laboratory. I began to realize that there is a common thread in a trauma and the method of learning at

Lakeside Lab. Both are Experiential Learning and both change people's perception of their ecology. I asked Bob about it.

BOB: Experiential learning differs from traditional learning because the outcome is not known ahead of time. In a traditional classroom there is a predictable outcome because lesson plans are designed to prove an idea, not test an idea. In the field, students don't set out to prove but rather to test an idea or hypothesis to see if it is true or not. Sometimes the experience comes out the way they expect it to, sometimes not.

EMILY: Life's that way too. Relationships aren't predictable either. A change in one affects all.

* * *

Life is lived in transition. The traditional way was to see it as a linear journey, with accepted times to go to school, marry, have children, and work at a career until it was considered time to step aside at retirement age. I don't think it ever really was like that. I think a lot of people who lived that way on the outside were faking it and many were actually living double lives, if not physically then certainly in their hearts. Life is actually cyclical. We repeat our patterns, but at different stages we are actually different people so we are shaped differently by them. Experiential learning is ongoing.

Because of the way people there shared their knowledge with me, I was better able to understand how scientific studies are now showing that there is a biological basis for Virginia Satir's observation that therapeutic methods which destroy the client's self-esteem are destructive. Results of a study supported by a grant from the UCLA Neuropsychoimmunology Task Force, chaired by Norman Cousins, show actual long-term physical changes in the number and effectiveness of Natural Killer cells of the immune system that correlated with mood changes. Working with a group of patients who had recently been told they had cancer, they found that as stress was released and a person became more positive and accepting of the problem, the number and effectiveness of the immune cells increased and continued to increase even more as time went on.

Dr. Matthew Friedman and scientists working at the National Center for Post Traumatic Stress Disorder (PTSD) at Yale have also found evidence of cellular changes in response to a person's emotional state. They observed cellular changes in the brain in response to trauma. The concept of cellular changes in brain cells taking place after birth (neural plasticity) is new and flies in the face of traditional thinking. But, with the advances in sophisticated equipment to observe and even take pictures of the brain, evidence of it is now indisputable. Dr. Friedman explains that irregularities and abnormalities occur in three areas of the brain system of people suffering from PTSD. (1) The locus ceruleus, which regulates the brain's secretion of hormones that mobilize the body for an emergency, becomes overactive. Once the locus ceruleus becomes overactive, it secretes too much of these brain chemicals—even in situations that are not serious. (2) After a trauma, another hormone that mobilizes the body to respond to emergencies, CRF (corticotrophin-releasing factor), seems to alert the body for emergencies that are not really there. (3) In response to trauma, the opiate system of the brain becomes hyperactive. This blocks out pain, but it also is probably the basis for one of the very serious PTSD symptoms: problems in personal relationships. It may be the cause of the emotional numbing (the inability to experience tender feelings) that is so often a part of PTSD. The research is exciting and opens all sorts of doors of hope for the future. We now know that our brains produce chemicals that control our moods, productivity, and behavior; our thoughts, based on our perceptions, trigger what chemicals are produced; we can learn to recognize the signs that indicate that the levels of chemicals in our brain are out of normal balance; and we can learn what our options are for restoring them to the normal balance.

Drug therapy (chemical injections or ingestion) can temporarily correct the imbalance but that only buys time to work on the problem. Except in cases of an injured or inadequately developed brain, external chemicals or surgery usually only deal with the symptoms, not the cause. The root of the problem lies in our thoughts and our perceptions because they're what trigger the production of our body's internal chemicals. Studies have shown that hope, or lack of hope, regulates what chemicals the brain produces. For instance, the neuromessenger serotonin has been implicated in mood disorders, (including the mood disorder obsessive-compulsive disorder, which many people think is the basis for our country's drug problem), anxiety disorders, violence, suicide, and schizophrenia. Judicial institutions and law enforcement agencies must deal with the violence. Morgues must deal with the suicides. These are the symptoms, not the underlying problem.

The help that is available for people who are hurting because of emotions after a trauma is based on new information and was not available to victims, including suicide victims, in the past. It is now. In the past, many people were driven to commit suicide by subliminal messages they were not aware of on the conscious level. It was not an issue of morals, will power, or conscious decision but an issue of physical chemicals stimulating receptor sites below the surface of conscious minds.

Suicide is a permanent solution to a temporary problem. New information made available by computer-assisted diagnostic equipment makes it possible for people to realize there is a reason for their suicidal thoughts that can be corrected. Now, depressed people have other options. Chemical imbalances can now be seen on a computer screen. A chemical imbalance in our bodies can be returned to normal or, in some cases, made normal for the first time. For example, by immediately using external drugs to get serotonin in balance it is possible to buy time to correct the cause of the disregulation. Certain cells in our bodies secrete chemicals in response to stimuli. These stimuli can be physical (like an injury or disease), external (like an event) or internal (like a thought). These cells do not know the difference between reality and our perception of reality. They respond only to our thoughts and attitudes, which are our perceptions of reality. Drugs only mask the underlying cause but they can be very important—or even essential—because they can buy time to treat the cause.

A SEROTONIN IMBALANCE DISCOVERED FROM AN AUTOPSIED BRAIN AFTER A SUICIDE COMES TOO LATE TO BE USEFUL TO THE VICTIM.

We have a right to relief from chemicals that are causing an imbalance and a right to bring them into balance in order to live happier and more productive lives. Because our bodies' opiates shield out part of our reality, we need help to do this. Opiates make it physically impossible for us to see the full picture, so we need to hook up with someone who can. It must be someone who understands the new discoveries. Approaches based on a foundation of the information compiled before the discovery of our bodies' natural opiates are obsolete and can be extremely counterproductive—or even dangerous.

Each person is different. Therefore, care must be taken to find the proper mesh when choosing an approach to healing. Unlike Hawaiian moo-moos, one size does not fit all. I needed different approaches at different times in my transition from the shock stage of trauma back to my goal of living in reality. As I grew through new experiences, my awareness and needs changed. Because I am an author, one of the approaches that was effective for me was putting my feelings down on paper in writing. It was one of the first tools used to help me release emotions still stored in my body from past events.

Chapter XX

SELF-REPAIR OF THE EQUIPMENT

New scientific discoveries are now pointing out the importance of self-maintenance and self-repair of the equipment. It is indisputably confirming that individual choice is the only effective tool to maintaining balance in our own lives. Balance is what keeps our wheel of life running smoothly. We are what we think; what we think determines what we choose.

Humans can choose which topics to focus thinking on, and for how long. A human is not a machine. A human *has* a machine that carries out instructions of his or her brain. These two concepts are entirely different. Peace and harmony come from choosing to keep mind, body and soul in balance. We can choose how long—and deeply—we think about each area.

Awareness of what neuromessengers the brain produces in response to stimuli of either external events or internal thoughts are influencing the content of our owner's manual. New discoveries about the chemicals that excite or inhibit our brain's reaction to stimuli are becoming the foundation upon which a revised owner's manual is being based.

We are learning now that it is possible to control the type and amount of mood-altering chemicals produced by our bodies. As with any of the other mood-altering drugs, however, our body's internally produced drugs (endorphins, enkephelens and other opiates) can be abused. Runner's high and other highs resulting from chemicals produced in our bodies during physical activity can become a means to an end in themselves.

We all need physical activity to keep our joints limber and keep adequate oxygen flowing through our bodies. Without exercise our brains and muscles become starved for oxygen and have to reduce productivity, but where does healthy physical exercise cross the line over to drug abuse? The answer, as with any other drug abuse (whether street drug or prescription drug) is when it becomes a shield to block us from feelings and allows us to deny and avoid pain of conflict our bodies are trying to resolve.

The mind must be fueled with reality. The body must be fueled with the proper nutrients—in the proper balance. The soul must be fueled with connection—both to the physical spirits in our everyday world and the unseen spirits and beliefs that influence our lives.

Because of our body's ability to produce chemicals to temporarily protect us from reality that is above the threshold of what we can bear, our mind travels in and out of reality. Our reality-torpedo does not follow a straight path. That's okay, because that's the way it is designed. Life is not all pleasure, or quick fixes for pain. If life were always sunny, it would soon be as parched as a desert. We need contrast.

Many of us in today's world are in, or have gone through, a period of spiritual bankruptcy. We feel disconnected from anything significant in life, from emotional meaning, or from worth. The area of the body has loomed far out of proportion. Our concentration is entirely focused on surrounding ourselves with objects that make us feel good, or on generating a desired physical response. As we concentrate on ingesting or injecting certain chemicals, devouring food, or getting good feelings from certain physical acts, the other points of the wheel are forgotten. For instance, sex can become a sport to generate good feelings rather than an act to express feeling of love and caring between two people.

Spirituality and religion are two different things. Spirituality is our connection with an unseen spirit. Religion is how we practice our spirituality. Like many individuals in today's world, many churches have gone spiritually bankrupt. Instead of the emphasis being on spirituality, the emphasis is on control. In our search for spirituality in such churches we end up confused because what is being publicly said is not what is being practiced. The foundation of spirituality is self-to-self connection. It requires us to say Aye-Aye to our I.I.—our Inner Intelligence.

A wealth of emotions and information is stored inside us all. Some believe it is biologically imprinted in our cells and has been carried down through the ages. Spirituality involves allowing ourselves to feel, and react to, a connection with these feelings and this information. When we put too little concentration on—or completely deny existence of—this inner spirituality, our wheel gets out of balance. Life gets bumpy.

Among other things, we put a layer of corrosion over the capacity to recognize or feel earned shame. It is important to make a distinction between earned shame and unearned shame. Some individuals, organizations and societies use shame as their major tool of control. This is often unearned shame imposed in response to manmade rules designed to fill their own needs.

Earned shame is shame felt as a consequence of behaviors that violate reality. All behaviors have consequences. All causes have effects. Shame is a necessary part of our lives. It is not meant to be a tool of exterior control. Rather, it is a buoy needed by our servomechanism to warn of outer limits of reality beyond which we may not go if we are to live our lives as a celebration. Reaching the outer limits of our possibilities, expanding our minds, bodies and souls (and thereby our harmony and happiness) to their fullest capacities depends not only on guidance in what to do but also in what not to do. Though sometimes confused, shame and humility are not the same thing. Humility is the acceptance that our mind is not in control of life. Reality (truth) is in control of life. Controlling our thinking does not control reality nor control cause and effect. Reality does. I believe in the Power of Positive Thinking. I do not believe in the power of wishful thinking.

Without humility, we cannot reach our full power. Too much energy is diverted to trying to control people around us and trying to control things around us. In a system based on control, rules and rituals are based on the needs of those in authority rather than on the needs and responsibilities of the individual. The needs of the ones in authority set the standards. In a system based on communication and caring, individual needs are examined and negotiated. However, though this system gives individuals more involvement in getting personal needs met, it also requires more personal acceptance of responsibility. Benefits rely on people making decisions and taking action. Individuals take an active role in keeping balance in their own lives.

People who do not need to accept responsibility for needs in their society often overlook the need to accept responsibility in the area of their own health. Research is now showing the advantage of taking more responsibility in choosing to get directly involved with such decisions. New scientific research is uncovering many areas where the mind/body connection exists. In these areas, our ability to choose is an active influence in self-repair of the equipment. As the mind becomes aware of the new information, decisions can be made and action taken.

The 1977 study by R. W. Bartrop and co-workers in New South Wales, Australia, was the first to show a measurable weakening of the human body's defense system following severe psychological stress in a real life setting. It laid the groundwork for many studies of how the brain, body and personal relationships are intertwined. Traditionally it was thought that reactions and attitudes in a person's relationships and social life had little to do with disease. However, with new information of how the brain actually works, evidence is growing that physical diseases are linked to our changing beliefs about ourselves, to the quality of our relationships, and to our position in our own social world. Our lungs, hearts and stomachs are not independent. They are linked together. They communicate chemically and are controlled by the brain.

Our tendency toward social connection may keep us well. In a study done at the Mt. Sinai School of Medicine, men who were married to women with terminal breast cancer showed a drop in responsiveness of lymphocytes, (blood cells of the immune system), immediately after their wives' deaths. Between four and fourteen months after the death, as their bereavement diminished, the immune functioning recovered. Questions scientists are trying to find the answer to are: What is the connection between grief and the immune system? Is the drop in responsiveness of lymphocytes due to a change in routine during grieving, such as nutrition, exercise, activity, or is it a response by the cells of the immune system to chemical signals from the central nervous system?

Luckily, new discoveries are suggesting steps that we ourselves can take to alter the way our immune system works. Using computers, scientists are now able to examine our physical bodies in much greater detail than they could before. They are making computer printouts of connections between cells, organs and systems previously undiscovered. This new information sheds a different light on the body of information they already knew and accepted.

Scientists are now able to move beyond the earlier, simplistic medical view of the body being made up of autonomous organs. While our organs have autonomous functions, they are not self-governing. There is mounting evidence that both emotional and physical disease is linked to our changing concept of ourselves, the relationships we choose, and how closely we relate to others.

On July 19, 1990, a year after the crash of United Flight 232, Harry Martens, a 79-year-old man from Elkhart, Indiana, suffered a stroke while in Sioux City to attend the memorial service for his wife and other victims of the tragedy. He and Olga Martens, 75, had married in 1937 and worked together on church-sponsored relief in North America, Europe, Asia, the Middle East and Latin America. From 1967 to 1969, the couple worked with the Mennonite Central Committee in the Jordan River valley on the West Bank. On the day of the tragedy, she had been flying back to Indiana after visiting their son and his family in Denver. On the morning of the anniversary, Harry had attended a breakfast for survivors and their families and families of victims. He and one of their daughters, who had accompanied him to Sioux City, planned to meet the others again at the airport at the time of day the crash had occurred. Instead, Martens was admitted to a Sioux City hospital early in the afternoon, before the start of the 4 p.m. memorial service in honor of the 112 who died. He died days later.

His lungs, heart and internal organs didn't stop functioning because they remembered the horrible catastrophe of a year ago that day. They got their instructions from Home Office—the Brain. Research is now showing that physical and psychological upsets cause the brain to produce powerful chemicals that alter our bodies' functions.

What Bartrop's New South Wales study found, and was able to measure, was a lower activity level of the T-Cells. T-Cells are thought to be derived from white blood cells that have migrated from bone marrow to the thymus gland. They attack foreign invaders in the blood steam. Blood has two basic parts: blood cells, also called blood corpuscles; and plasma, the fluid in which blood cells are suspended. T-Cells circulate in this blood system and fight to destroy anything that the body recognizes as something harmful.

It now appears likely that cells of the immune system are equipped to respond to chemical signals from the central nervous system, the CNS. Connections between the nervous system and the immune system seem to allow the mind to influence resistance or susceptibility to illness. Networks of nerve endings have now been found in the thymus gland, a gland in the chest that plays a key role in immunity. They've been found in the lymphatic system, which consists of lymph gland or nodes found throughout the body that produce lymphocytes, a type of white blood cell that attacks intruder cells. They're in the spleen, which modifies the blood, and the marrow inside bones that produces most of the blood cells, including all of the red cells and most of the white cells.

Receptor sites have now been found on lymphocytes for neuroendocrines, neurotransmitters and neuropeptides. It is now thought that the chemicals that plug into these sites stimulate decisions of what kind of cells are produced, their migration and their activity. During stress beyond our ability to handle easily the SNS, (Sympathetic Nervous System), is activated. This increases the level of circulating hormones that suppress immune function.

Decisions that our mind makes that affect the balance in our lives may not always be in the emotional area. They may be decisions in the area of the body—decisions on what foods we choose to eat or not eat. In Africa, Asia, and Central and South America millions of children are going blind and dying. Children with severe vitamin A deficiency develop xerophthalmia, a disorder of the cornea that leads to night blindness and eventually total blindness. The disorder is linked with illnesses like diarrhea, measles and pneumonia, which are major killers of Third World children. It is suspected that a lack of vitamin A may weaken the linings of respiratory and intestinal tracts, allowing viruses and bacteria that cause pneumonia and diarrhea to get a foothold.

Yet almost everywhere this situation is found there is vitamin A in abundance—in fruits and in green and yellow vegetables. If these children were simply fed a diet including these foods, they could get all of the vitamin they need. In Indonesia, papaya fruit, which is rich in vitamin A, is grown for export to other countries. Few Indonesians eat it. In the Philippines, some parents are wary of giving their children vegetables because they believe they are unhealthy for children. In Africa, many people eat a lot of the right plants but eat no oil, even though Africa is a big exporter of vegetable oils. The body can't use the vitamin A in plants unless some fat is eaten along with it.

Whereas, in the past, symptoms of emotions after a trauma were often looked upon as somewhat of a matter of choice on the part of the patient or a moral issue suggesting a lack of submission to strict spiritual rituals, scientists and patients alike are now understanding and approaching the problem from the physical basis. Both scientists and patients are realizing that depression after a trauma is not something to just tough out. No matter what the cause, the symptoms are something to be taken seriously by both patients and doctors.

Although feelings of depression are normal after a trauma, they may also be caused by physical reasons. As with any symptoms, it is necessary to determine whether the cause is emotional or physical. If it is caused by a physical problem, solve the physical problem and the depression goes away. In his book *The Good News About Depression* Dr. Mark Gold says there are as many as 75 hidden physical causes of on-going, unexplained depression. A leading American health magazine, *Prevention* lists some major physical causes of depression.

Drugs prescribed to fight depression may have a side-effect of causing depression in some people. These drugs will not affect all people that way, but they will affect some, and it may not show up right away. It could take months to a year before the symptoms are noticeable.

Thyroid problems are a major cause of depression. Fortunately, there are simple blood tests for detecting problems in thyroid function.

Most women suffer some form of depression during or just prior to menstruation. Body chemicals are associated with mood change during this time, as they are during menopause, use of oral contraceptives or after just having a baby. Symptoms may include mood swings, food cravings, crying, emotional withdrawal and insomnia.

Insulin delivers sugar throughout the body. When too little insulin is produced, or when the body is unable to use it properly, sugar builds up in the blood instead of reaching the cells where it is needed for energy. Symptoms which may be thought to be caused by depression (low energy, fatigue and sleeplessness) may actually be caused by diabetes.

Inadequate food intake will cause depression. People who go on rapid weight loss diets that leave them hungry put themselves at risk. Inadequate nutrient intake can lead to nutrient deficiencies.

People with low activity levels are at significantly greater risk for depression than those with high levels. On the brighter side, researchers of the California Department of Health Services found that when couch potatoes finally do start exercising, they are less likely to have symptoms of depression.

Dr. Dan Oren, a senior clinical investigator in the clinical psychobiology branch of the National Institute of Mental Health reports that millions of Americans suffer because of a sunlight deficiency caused by too little sunlight in the fall and winter. Symptoms can often be relieved by light therapy, exposure to regular sessions of bright, full-spectrum light.

Animal studies have shown that if complex carbohydrates like rice, bread and cereal are always eaten with protein, there might be risk of mild depression. This may be because the amino acids in protein prevent tryptophan from getting into the brain. Tryptophan is essential for producing serotonin, the brain chemical that keeps moods stable. Author Judith Wurtman, of *Managing Your Mind And Mood Through Food* believes that, when eaten alone, complex carbohydrates boost serotonin production in the brain. This does not apply to fruits because they contain simple sugars, which don't stimulate serotonin release.

Stress is a major cause of muscle tension. A stressful thought or event can initiate the nervous system's well known fight-or-flight response. Neuromessengers transmit the message "tighten" to the muscles. The brain's message "produce exciter chemicals such as adrenaline" is triggered. The body tenses. Tension is preparation for action. Each time the body's awareness, decision to take action, action cycle is interrupted before the action stage, clenched muscles and tension remain. Over a period of time, this causes blood vessels to constrict, decreasing blood flow. The muscles become starved for oxygen and transmit signals of pain. Sometimes this happens suddenly. A muscle spasm can transmit sudden, painful signals to the brain, which then contracts blood vessels. Until the muscles relax, pain restricts movement and activity. If this tension in the muscles is not released, they can knot up into hard lumps called trigger points. Not all muscle tension is caused by emotional stress. Again, checking to find the real cause is essential. Other possibilities include bad posture which can result in cramping and muscle fatigue. Work habits such as hunching over a computer for extended periods without taking breaks to release accumulating tension contribute. Inadequate nutrients, such as from a low-calcium diet, is thought to cause muscle cramps. So is a sedentary lifestyle which includes little exercise, the natural tranquilizer.

The body is designed to release tension during the contraction and release of exercise such as competitive sports or a long walk in the hills. Also needed in combination with these aerobic exercises are exercises that gently stretch muscles to keep them limber. Once a muscle spasms, however, stretching is not recommended as it can make matters worse.

Any of the methods effective in relieving stress can help prevent muscle tension. People are different, and therefore react to the various types of therapy differently. Meditation, progressive relaxation, visualization, selective awareness exercises, biofeedback training and massage all are effective in helping people become aware of their body's tension signals.

Massage can loosen and relax tense muscles by increasing blood flow, but it can also aggravate an injury, trauma or inflamed area. It is absolutely necessary to be sure a person is knowledgeable in this field, knows the difference, and knows your personal medical history before giving a massage.

The following tension zones have been identified:

HEAD: Although the cause of tension headaches is not yet known, some people theorize that the tension may be in the scalp muscles. Relaxation techniques seem to help.

FACE: Tension can build in the facial muscles when we express emotions and smile, frown, scowl, wrinkle the nose or grimace. A relaxation technique is taking a deep breath and letting it out slowly.

TONGUE AND JAW: A relaxed tongue lays in the bottom of the mouth when it's not talking. Like all joints in the body, the jaw rests on a pad of cartilage. If jaw muscles are always tight, they wear away the cartilage. Jaw tension as well as tension that shows up as clenching and grinding of teeth, can cause symptoms such as headaches, earaches and dull, aching facial pain. Because this tension can also be caused by a bad bite, a dentist may suggest orthodontic work or wearing an orthodontic appliance during sleep. Stretching while breathing can ease mild tension. Open the mouth wide, without forcing, while breathing deeply, then close the mouth while exhaling slowly and massaging the muscles over the jaw hinge.

Research studies have documented a relationship between exposure to various forms of stressful life experiences and changes in the immune system in both animals and humans. A study supported by a task force at UCLA found tangible, verifiable changes in the cells of the immune system of patients who had been newly diagnosed with a very serious type of cancer, malignant melanoma, after participating in six weeks of group sessions. It was designed to observe what processes took place in a patient's immune system in response to a diagnosis of cancer, and if helping a person to deal with the emotions after a diagnosis could have a beneficial effect on the processes.

The study found that, after hearing the diagnosis, fewer cells of the immune system were produced, a lower percentage of natural killer cells (NK cells) of the immune system were produced, and that there was impaired activity of the NK cells that were produced. After the intervention, patients showed lower depressed and anxious mood states, but more anger. The scientists think this indicates that patients who give themselves permission to be angry utilize the tools of positive assertiveness and defiance rather than irritability or rage.

The information scientists are collecting for an owner's manual for self-maintenance and self-repair of our equipment seems to be understandable and usable!

Chapter XXI

DEVISING A CAMPAIGN STRATEGY: THERAPIES AND APPROACHES

The first thing that must be done to relieve pain first noticed after a trauma, as in the diagnosis of any other pain-producing problem, is to determine whether the cause is functional or organic. This means:

Is it a result of emotions stored after a trauma. . .

Or a physical injury received during the crisis. . .

Or, perhaps, a natural impairment?

Minimal brain injury in disasters is sometimes overshadowed by the emotional impact of the crisis. In addition, caution is urged by Dr. Wayne H. Peterson of Phoenixville, Pennsylvania, because of the similarities in symptoms of epileptic disorder seizures and seizures like some caused by the psychological trauma of post traumatic stress. Common symptoms he points out include amnesia, auditory hallucinations, dissociation and psychosis-like experiences. If misdiagnosed, untreated seizures can complicate the treatment for emotions, resulting in treatment failure, or repeated entries into the mental health care system.

The next step is to determine if the person is a linear or global thinker and if the person collects information predominantly by audio or visual means. To be effective, treatment approaches for each of these categories of thinkers must be an entirely different mix. With therapy approaches, unlike Hawaiian moo-moos, one size does not fit all. An approach must be designed that is a tailored blend of techniques to fit the needs of the person who is hurting. It is necessary to realize that people may be expressing the same pain, only expressing it differently. The person who is hurting must be a partner in designing the approach because it is important to match the type of therapy with the way the person with the problem processes information. Global thinkers see the whole picture as one unit. Linear thinkers see each part of the jigsaw puzzle as individual pieces. Until they get all their ducks lined up in a row, they can't see the picture.

Global thinkers see the forest rather than the trees. It can aggravate a global thinker if someone *insists* on talking about one magnolia tree. "What magnolia tree? Why doesn't he talk about the topic we're supposed to be concentrating on, the forest, instead of talking about some magnolia tree?"

Linear thinkers, on the other hand, can get overwhelmed by the quacking of a whole pen full of ducks. They have to let one duck out of the gate and on to the path, understand that problem, then let the second one out. All ducks must be out and in a row to see a natural solution.

I am a visual-global thinker. I can only write little books because my writing room isn't large enough for me to spread out the pages of a long book. I live in a five-level, soon-to-be century-old house, with the high ceilings, stained glass windows and parquet floors that were common in Victorian houses of that era. Way up at the top was a ballroom accessible only through the servant's quarters. Stories have it that it was used as a secret hiding place during prohibition days.

Well, it's not prohibition days now, so I climb way up there to write my books. I can see forever in the winter time when the leaves are off the forty-foot trees outside. I can see off to a distant point where the sun sets in a big orange ball behind the snow-covered Loess Hills. In the summer, enclosed in my private forest, the curved glass of the turret windows make me feel like I'm writing in a bird nest.

Across the floor marches a more-or-less orderly procession of manila folders holding copies of research reports. On top, and extending down like a computer software pull-down menu, the chapters grow. In one corner are my computer, reference books, tape recorder, and VCR for viewing reference tapes. In every other available space—on the couches, on the chests and up the walls on bulletin boards—are little scraps of paper, magazines, notes on restaurant napkins, and anything else that I happened to capture thoughts on during the time I've been writing on the subject.

It's all clear to me. I know, and can see in my mind, what's in every pile—even in every level of every pile. I'm very comfortable in this room, but it drives linear thinkers nuts! As an author, I don't interview linear thinkers in this room. I interview linear thinkers downstairs on the first floor, sitting on matching couches in one of the two formal living rooms. The nine-foot mirror with its columns, the paneled entry hall, its carved staircase and crystal chandelier are all evidence that some linear thinker Victorian lady or gentlemen who designed it a hundred years ago was comfortable with ducks in a row.

To be most effective when I interview people for my books, I understand the importance of matching the type of setting with the type of thinker. It's just as important to match the type of therapy approach with the type of thinker. Therapy approaches may be grouped into seven broad categories:

INWARD LOOKING: Psychoanalysis relies on insights gained by exploring things that happened in the past. Cognitive Therapy emphasizes changing how we think about our troubles.

BEHAVIORAL THERAPY: addresses actions we can take to cope with our problems more effectively.

FAMILY/SYSTEMS APPROACH: examines effects of learned habits, roles, and reactions to opinions of others. It holds that no problems are individual, that all reflect a malfunction in the family or system as a unit. It examines how the parts of the system interact, and resembles cultural anthropology which explores the way beliefs are transmitted from generation to generation.

DESENSITATION: emphasis re-learning responses by re-experiencing emotions in safe, controlled settings.

FLOODING: helps patients release stored tension by reliving the trauma in detail.

ELECTROCONVULSIVE TREATMENT: uses a fairly strong but brief electrical current passed directly through a person's brain to induce a seizure, which some think has the effect of helping to bring severely depressed patients back to normal.

PSYCOPHARMOCOLOGY: seeks to correct chemical imbalances by identifying and adjusting for psychological or underlying biological dysfunction. This is seldom used alone. If the cause is physical, it buys time to work on the psychological basis of the problem. If the problem is behavioral, the person usually still needs help in adjusting to life and to change habits.

BODY APPROACHES: may concentrate on movement, exercise, body alignment, or integration of mind and body by teaching flexibility, relaxation, muscle tone or body awareness.

Tension in muscles is a preparation for action, a preparation to respond. When the mind denies and avoids stimuli too painful to handle at the moment, it also blocks the appropriate activity of response. Rather than being released, tension accumulates with each new stressful incident. Therapies that concentrate on movement allow tension accumulated in muscles to be released through physical activity. Like drug therapy (other than drug therapy used to correct a physically-based chemical imbalance) it cannot be used alone because it doesn't deal with the cause, only the symptom. Also, as is true with external drugs, bodies can become dependent on these chemicals produced internally during physical activity, urging for the pleasure of higher and higher levels of "runner's high." This needs to be closely monitored, both in movement therapy and in sports.

Some Experiential Education programs focus on movement, exercise and the body approach. Experiential Educators are *educators*, they are not *therapists*. These are two different fields. However, each must draw heavily on the principles of the other to be effective. The door to new awareness can be opened by education, exercise or medicine in the context of the whole person. Professionally, the three young ladies who live with me, Dawn Snyder, Colleen Henry and Karen Dionne each use different approaches. Dawn is employed by the county as County Naturalist. She designs and conducts field trips into natural areas for both children and adults. Her approach is to hike people through the woods, or into the lakes, to expose them to experiences that will help them discover how nature must remain in balance in order to exist. As humans, we are governed by the same rules. Colleen is a Health Promotion Coordinator. She teaches the importance of exercise using the conventional organizational system of a hospital. She coordinates Health Promotion programs, not only for the employees of the hospital but for companies in the whole community. She says the thrust of the Health Promotion component of the hospital is to try to educate people on the importance of exercise, and on the physical and emotional health benefits of exercise. Colleen helps people learn about the body's ability to produce endorphins and about their natural, beneficial emotional high. Karen is a Physicians' Assistant in a private clinic. It is essential to determine whether emotions after a trauma have an emotional or physical cause. Karen's trained to check this out.

Flooding is a form of exposure therapy designed to push patients back into the traumatic experience, forcing them to confront their repressed anxieties and memories. It integrates two important parts of the traumatic memory, the mind's picture of what happened at the time and the highly charged emotions attached to it. The difference this time is that the person is going through the experience in a safe place with safe, supportive people near. The outcome is known. With repeated exposures, as with repeated lancings of a boil, the pain is released.

Behavioral Therapy is not new; the Ancient Romans had it figured out. They were practicing Behavioral Therapy when they put spiders in the cups of alcoholics. Behaviorists believe knowledge comes from experience. They refuse to deal with things such as thoughts which, in the past, could not be measured. However now, with the continuing advancements in diagnostic equipment, thoughts and mental concepts are becoming increasingly understandable. It has been obvious for a long time that humans are complex creatures with many parts—physical, intellectual and emotional. What has not been obvious until now, however, is that both physical parts and emotional processes are understandable and observable. In the past, emotional processes have been shrouded in mystery. Now, through the use of radioactive tracers and computerized equipment, these processes can be observed, and even photographed.

The Greek philosopher Epictetus taught that men are disturbed not by events but by their *perception* of events. That idea is the basis of Cognitive Therapy. Instead of examining suppressed thoughts, cognitive therapists examine a hurting person's conscious thoughts. The problem with using this form of therapy as an exclusive form is that one can't examine conscious thoughts until they become conscious. As long as the opiate system has them blocked out, they are useless in Cognitive Therapy.

Behavioral Therapy and Cognitive Therapy share the common conviction that most psychological problems are more straightforward than medical or psychoanalytic professionals believe.

The medical profession approaches the problem of hurting people with a focus on external solutions: prescribing external medicines or performing surgery. Traditionally, they have paid little attention to the processes of emotions and have considered them a mystery. At points in some people's emotional journey from trauma to acceptance, it can be absolutely necessary to use external chemicals to correct a chemical imbalance. When the body itself is incapable of producing the right chemicals, in the right amounts, it needs, and deserves, help. As a rule, though, the role of external drugs is to treat the symptoms, not the cause. External drugs buy time. Time is needed to change one's perceptions. If the cause of the problem is not resolved, inner conflict and tension will remain.

Psychotherapy is therapy using verbal methods. Many people still confuse psychotherapy with psychoanalysis. When the word psychotherapy is mentioned, many people still think of spending years in sessions on a couch delving into dark secrets of the past. These pictures are images of Freud's psychoanalysis, which is just one type of psychotherapy, and an increasingly less-used type. Freudian therapists are non-directive. They do not analyze, but rather act as a sound board. They believe that as the client focuses on memories in the past, body memories are released and recalled. The patient talks randomly. The therapist does not offer advice, but relies on the patient's insight.

Psychoanalysis focuses on examining things that happened in the past and on trying to figure out how these experiences are influencing how we think about things in the present. This is an extremely important piece of the puzzle of Post Traumatic Stress, but it is only one piece, no longer the whole picture. It never was but, before the discovery of receptor sites in the brain for opiates, psychoanalysts didn't know that. The trend today is toward shorter-term, goal-oriented treatment.

It is vital for a person to understand why he or she acts in a certain way, but *Awareness* is only the first of three steps of change. We cannot stop after the first step. The second step, *Decision* comes after we become aware of an event, (or a belief in a life rule we have been taught), that is influencing us to behave in a way that is messing up our lives. We must then make a conscious decision to change the way we react to that stimulus. Unless we decide to change, we will not change.

Action is the third step.

Chapter XXII

PEACE NEGOTIATIONS: THE GRIEF PROCESS

To change our perceptions, we must go back and look at our past experiences. We now have more mature eyes and understanding than we had at the time of past traumas. We will see the event more accurately. This is the only way to change a false perception of past events, or to emotionally accept a true perception that our mind has been anesthetizing us from fully seeing. False perceptions must be changed to an understanding of what really happened (to reality) before we can gain the inner peace to become happier and more productive people. We only have so much energy, no more. In order to reach, or even recognize, our full potential or set and achieve goals at our highest capabilities, we can't waste part of it. As long as we must use part of this energy, (perhaps even most of this energy), to fight an inner battle raging silently and unrecognized within our bodies, our success in life is limited by a glass ceiling. The freedom from pain we gain after recognizing the symptoms, facing the demon, and overcoming the emotions stored after a trauma is the tool to shatter this glass ceiling.

Scientists are working hard to help people who are hurting find new ways to recognize and deal with symptoms of post traumatic stress. Much of their work is focused in the areas of depression, addiction and criminal behavior. These problem areas seem to be associated with a chemical change that affects the way the body functions.

We're all riding on a train together, because tragedy and the resulting post traumatic stress can strike by day or night. Neither respects age, income or nationality and each can affect the way men, women and children see life. This train runs on a circular track. It needs to stop at stations to pick up professionals, but it also needs to stop at stations to pick up people who are hurting. Both are needed. Ordinary people do not learn about trauma in a laboratory. They learn about it during a trauma. Based on their experiences, professionals then set up lab studies to learn how to help bring relief. Professionals and people who are hurting must work as an interdependent team. Each group contributes information of equal importance to bring current awareness to a higher level.

What is becoming perfectly clear from current research is that trauma causes disillusionment and loss and that there is no hope for the future until acceptance of that disillusionment and loss. After a tragedy, life, as we had experienced it until then, is no longer reality. For a while our mind tries to continue in the old life, but that life has become simply an illusion. As our conscious mind reacts to the illusion and our body chemicals react to life as it is now, confusion generates stress. It's a painful time and, when the pain gets too intense, our opiate system kicks in to protect us. The normal balance of our body chemicals gets out of balance.

The experience that changes our perception, and therefore our thoughts, of the trauma is the grief process. We must grieve the loss of our shattered dreams and expectations. We must face the reality, and the pain, that our lives are not the same as they were before the physical or emotional trauma. The process is painful. The reason our mind blocked out the full impact of the situation in the first place was because it was too painful for us to handle all at once. It isn't any less painful during the grief process. The difference, however, is that with help we can go at our own pace the second...and third...time around. We can experience the pain in small doses that will not overwhelm us. This process is called desensitization. Because of the way the opiate system works to numb our pain, it is usually not one a person can do alone. Group support supplies the element of realistic thinking and hope.

When we ride the train on the journey through the grief process, it stops at stations of many therapies. The grief process utilizes different approaches at different stages of its journey of growth from loss of illusions to acceptance of reality. Going through the grief process takes time. It is painful, but it is worth it. Only when our mind, body and soul are in balance can we live without conflict. Only when what our mind is aware of, the messages that our body's chemicals are transmitting, and what we're experiencing emotionally are the same do we feel peace and harmony. Like a tire with a boot on it, when one of these three points is out of balance, our life runs bumpy.

One will not submit to pain of the grief process until pain of the symptoms is greater. When a person who is hurting becomes aware that these pains are simply clues that lead to unblocking the chemical molecules of emotion, hope kicks in. Hope then becomes the engine that keeps him or her going through the process of grief. HOPE is the KEY to P-T-S-D.

Awareness is the first step to reconciling the loss of how life was before the trauma. Suppressing the reality of the loss prevents us from confronting it so we can experience the pain and release it. While this denial plays an important role, even an essential role for a while, eventually the grief process must start.

All grief must be experienced—and then must end.

There are risks, however, to ending grief. There is an element of fear involved in giving up the illusion of the old life—fear of what the future holds. Fear of the future can hold us in bondage to the past, hold us in a fantasy bond that prevents us from experiencing happiness in the present. Thus the **FIRST** stage of grief, **DENIAL AND AVOIDANCE,** is a beneficial one, but taking too long to make the decision to move on through the other steps can turn it into a quagmire. When hope cracks the door to the future open a little bit, anger is the first feeling that comes through it, anger at the injustice. My thoughts were: "I didn't deserve this; Life isn't fair; Why did this happen to me?"

The **SECOND** stage of grief, **ANGER**, is a stage of intense feelings—as well it should be if the loss was severe. Grief is not a blame game. This second stage is not an attempt to point a finger at someone or something and say "You caused it. You made a victim of me." True, we are victims, but concentrating on the role of someone or some thing outside ourselves at this point prevents us from concentrating on our feelings. Releasing, and thereby taking one step in relieving, post traumatic stress requires identifying and admitting feelings. As we successfully confront each intense feeling, others, recognizing our new strength, emerge into our conscious thought.

This leads into the **THIRD** step of grief, **CONFUSION**, a stage where hope is causing our brain to produce exciter neurotransmitters, and fear of pain is causing it to produce inhibitor neurotransmitters. As body memories, (memories stored as chemicals in our bodies), rise to the surface, thoughts of "Is this true?" "Did this really happen—or am I making this up?" "Am I going crazy?" plague us. Because our mind is no longer functioning as we are accustomed to, fear that we might be losing it is common at this stage of grief. Feedback from a professional is important. When necessary, the opiate system of our body works hard at this stage to protect us from reality. A supportive professional will work just as hard to steady us and help us confront the reality of the trauma, one small step at a time, until we grow strong enough to see the picture as a whole.

When we do grow strong enough to look at the whole picture, it is usually sad enough to trigger the **FOURTH** stage of grief, **DEPRESSION**. The sadness felt at this stage is not the same sadness as the depression produced by a chemical imbalance in the brain. Although feelings from both sources may run concurrently, the sadness of the fourth stage of grief is a response to realistically appraising a depressing situation, not simply an automatic reaction to a stimulus. In life, patches of sunshine and patches of rain alternate. Life is not meant to be all happiness. In a healthy life, there is a realistic balance. This is a time of experiencing the sadness of loss, a time for mourning broken dreams and unfulfilled expectations. It is a stage to close the door on the past, a quiet time to regain energy and become aware that it is possible to live in a future without chronic pain.

The people whose traumas are described in this book—Bob, Cricket, Liz, Colleen, Julia and the rest, have all experienced various steps of grief, sometimes in combination, on their body's own time schedule. There is no normal or appropriate length of time for grief to last. Grief lasts until the job is done.

Eventually, depression gently flows into the **FIFTH** step, **ACCEPTANCE**. We do not forget what has happened; we simply accept that trauma is an event, not a state of existence. As our thinking gets more in balance, our brain's production of neuromessengers gets more in balance. This is a stage in which we begin to make happy choices again, choices based on reality rather than on denial and avoidance. It's a time of opening the windows of our soul and letting the fresh, calm breeze of a new life blow in.

Neuromessengers help form the biological basis of behavior and moods. They are produced by our brains in response to a stimulus, either internal or external. Our thoughts play a major role in which ones are produced. We can control how long we allow thoughts to stay in our memories by consciously challenging unrealistic ones and reinforcing realistic ones. We can override the negative thought pathways grooved into our systems by past thoughts and experiences and replace them with positive thought pathways based on present day reality.

Changing from a negative attitude to a positive attitude, from a state of free-floating anxiety to calmness, from restlessness to inner peace, is not an event. It is a process. The process begins with hope—hope generated by awareness of other options than the ones we have been choosing either consciously or by surrendering to our inner silent dictator. Information to develop positive thought pathways constantly envelopes us. It's called reality. The problem is that as long as we are in the shock stage of trauma, our body's opiate system insulates us from the pain of our reality until we become strong enough to experience it. In the shock stage of trauma, our inner resources are in disarray, so our brains give us the opportunity to retreat and regroup.

Then, courage returns. Courage is faith—faith that we can change. Only when we have hope will our brain's toggle switch over from inhibitor neuromessengers to exciter neuromessengers. Only when we have hope will our brains produce chemicals that allow us to move to the next stages: DECISION and ACTION. Then, rebuilding can begin.

When the work of grief is done, it is possible to enter the mainstream of life again because emotions are no longer anesthetized. Feelings can flow naturally through the body. With the acceptance of reality that the trauma did actually happen comes the awareness that we no longer fit into our old perception of life. Grief changed me. I grew. There came a time when I began to question the routines I was following. It began one night when I had tickets to an annual concert I had gone to for years. But, because my writing time from 4 am to noon, I was tired. The conflict between my old life and my new life began to come into focus. The awareness came that some of the things I did were vestiges of my old life, and that I was still doing them out of routine.

I told myself: "Focus on this night, and this night only. Think about it and, more importantly, give yourself permission to experience the feelings released. Is going to that concert what you really feel like doing on this night? "

It really wasn't. I felt like going to sleep. I found it a very hard thing to do, but I went to sleep. I took a small step in detaching from the routine and confinement of my old life's rules.

I had withdrawal symptoms the next day from having broken away from a routine. I suddenly realized that I was in the grip of, and controlled by, things associated with the past that had supported me through a time of numbness, intense emotional pain, anger, fear and confusion. Still, this was progress. Whereas before I had been dependent on certain people, places, and things, now I was dependent on visual and emotional memories associated with those people, places, and things.

I realized I could take action to break this dependence. A dependence on flashbacks is easier to desensitize than a dependence on something in the present. Flashbacks are limited because they are not renewable. Each time a little of the pain is released, the balloon gets smaller. Finally, the memory is emotionally limp and empty. Although the memory remains, it no longer holds painful emotions.

Detachment does not come automatically. The decision to separate from a person or situation involves the pain of loss. The process of pulling apart is painful. A decision must be made to take action. Then, action must actually be taken in spite of awareness that the consequences of the action will be painful. The pain generated by detachment is temporary. The pain generated by an inner conflict between illusion and reality continues until a truce is negotiated. Eventually, I found that I was able to depend less on things associated with the past that had supported me through my painful time.

Grief is a period of flushing out numbness and negative emotions. Acceptance is a neutral time. The last step of re-entry is a time of action. It is a time of creativity. Trauma puts relationships, interests, routines and normal comings and goings into disarray. Setting new goals around a new work, a new idea, purpose, faith or love is the action that liberates the energy to get back on the highway of life.

Our brain rides a merry-go-round around a circle of connections between how we see ourselves, what we think, and what we do. After a trauma, when the brightly painted and decorated horses get weak and falter, the whole merry-go-round slows down. Even the music sounds funny. Life, at that moment, isn't so merry.

If, during a trauma, more exciter chemicals are produced than can ride along our Inner Interstate at that particular moment, some get blocked in the parking areas of the Inner Interstate rest stops along the way. However, just as a traveler is not meant to stay in the parking lot of an Interstate rest stop for an extended period of time, but only for the length of time needed for certain actions, these chemicals are meant to plug into their appropriate receptor sites when necessary, stimulate them, then continue their journey when the road is safe. Sometimes, because of the life's rules we have been taught by prior training and experience, it takes a long time for our brain to decide the road is safe.

The grief process is a tow truck we can call on when we need it. Because of the denial inherent in the shock stage of emotions after a trauma, we'll usually not be able to get going again without the help of a person who knows how to use the capabilities of the tow truck. It seldom does any good to decide to call a tow truck if we do not also make the decision to use the skills of its driver too. Grief takes us through the process from the shock stage of post traumatic stress to reality. It helps us travel through the denial that something so traumatic could actually happen in our lives to being able to face that it *did* happen. Our lifestyles *have* changed because of it but, in spite of it, we still have the strength to go on and build a new lifestyle.

We are what we think. The thoughts that come to our minds determine what we do at the moment and what we are able to accomplish. Reactions in a crisis are by reflex. They depend, to a great extend, on how our mind was trained before the crises to view such a situation.

In everyday life, too, our thoughts determine what we are able to accomplish. Every accomplishment starts with a thought in the brain. As it gains force, a thought becomes a dream, then moves on to become a goal. A goal is a dream with a deadline.

The next step is decision, a decision of whether or not to take action. In a catastrophe, the decision is automatic. We emotionally freeze or we take action. How we react depends on how our mind has molded beforehand. On the other hand, in everyday life there is time to analyze situations, consider options and choose a decision. The decision of whether or not to take action is a major fork in the road. If we decide to keep our dream to ourselves, that's what it remains—our dream. We keep it in our own brain. We control it. We allow it to have only the characteristics we want it to have—or need it to have. If we decide to take action we are, by this decision, also deciding to share our dream. We give up control, release it and let it take on a life of its own. Eventually, we become controlled by our dream or, as happens with people with a high self-image, learn to share control of our lives with our dream.

If we decide to take action, the level of challenge we decide to accept determines our level of accomplishment. We're not going to get to New York if we accept a ride on a train going to Los Angeles. The level of challenge we accept is determined by self-image. If we don't think we can accomplish a task, we'll not accept the challenge to try. We'll never accomplish tasks we don't try; only tasks we do try.

Whether or not we *think* we can accomplish a task determines what neuromessengers are produced. If we don't think we can do it, our brain produces inhibitor chemicals. Inhibitor chemicals give us a feeling of protection as they say "Come, let me put a protective shell around you for a while. There is emotional danger in trying this idea. For now, come rest in an Inner Interstate rest area parking lot until the danger has passed." On the other hand, if we think we can do it, our brain produces exciter chemicals. This gives us a feeling of energy, a mood of "Let's get going and travel the Inner Interstate hand-in-hand with this idea and see how far we can go!"

In our world today there are many people who have gone through trauma, either a sudden catastrophe or low level doses of trauma over an extended period of time. Some are people whose abilities are now stuck in an Inner Interstate rest area parking lot. They are members of the emotionally walking dead. They are not waiting for a tow truck to come tow them away to a permanent landfill, but for a tow truck driver to come help them replace life's rules that are no longer working for them with ones that are, to tune up their inner thoughts and get them back on a highway that leads to productivity and happiness.

Where are you along the highway to emotional health?

INDEX